EXPLORING THEMES IN THE CALENDAR OF THE SOUL

LUIGI MORELLI

EXPLORING THEMES IN THE CALENDAR OF THE SOUL

iUniverse books may be ordered through booksellers or by contacting:

iUniverse
1663 Liberty Drive
Bloomington, IN 47403
www.iuniverse.com
844-349-9409

EDITING: Kristine Hunt
BOOK COVER IMAGE: Sophie Bourguignon Takada (Calendar of the Soul: image for verse 1 of Easter)
COVER LAY-OUT AND GRAPHIC ART: Kim Govoni

ISBN: 978-1-6632-2534-4 (sc)
ISBN: 978-1-6632-2535-1 (e)

Print information available on the last page.

iUniverse rev. date: 09/29/2021

CONTENTS

INTRODUCTION

This study follows on my interest on and daily work with the Calendar of the Soul. The verses have been part of my meditative life at various points in my life. They have returned in strength since the summer of 2010. In stage after stage the regular meditation extended to working first with the complementary verse, then with the corresponding verses of the so-called quartets or crosses. The daily meditations were accompanied with contemplation of the artistic work on the verses by Anne Stockton and Karl König.

An important milestone in the formulation of living questions lay in the essays on the Calendar by Karl König, and among these the one on thinking and boding acquired a central place when I first read it some fifteen years ago.[1] Through it the division of the year in the two halves (spring and summer / fall and winter) started to acquire a deeper experiential dimension once I returned to the daily practice of the verses.

Over time I devised ways to carry awareness of the calendar verse over the day and to start observing the unfolding of my soul life and biography in relation to the verses. This was not a methodical journaling but rather a frequent collection of observations. I felt a deep inner connection with the calendar growing and influencing my life.

In the last two years the study accelerated. I started collecting daily notes on the week's verses and quartets and followed particular themes such as hope, memory, cosmic Word, warmth and heart, expressions of selfhood, beauty, and so on. In so doing I am continuing the thematic approach that Karl König takes in his commentaries. I expanded the

---

[1] Karl König, *Rudolf Steiner's Calendar of the Soul, a Commentary*, Rudolf Steiner Press, 1989.

study on pointed questions (e.g., cosmic Word, cosmic thinking, cosmic life, cardinal festivals corresponding to equinoxes and solstices) from the spiritual scientific revelations of Rudolf Steiner. Once again I went back to the work of Karl König, this time from an expanded publication than the one to which I had access at the beginning.[2] I am deeply indebted to his contributions, which form a constant backdrop to the present work.

The Origin of the Calendar

We know that Rudolf Steiner devoted a great part of the second stage of the development of the Anthroposophical Society (from about 1910 to 1916) to the new Christology. The period was inaugurated in 1909 with the revelations about the etheric Christ in our times. In the same year, Steiner spoke of the two Jesus children—the Solomon Jesus and the Nathan Jesus—in the lecture cycle on the Luke Gospel. And these revelations, which were already part of the Fifth Gospel, formed the prelude to the lectures that carried that name in the year 1913.

Central to the above impulse was also the publication of the *Calendar of the Soul* in 1912. The Calendar is a meditative path that unites microcosm and macrocosm. It portrays how the individual soul's path is affected by the macrocosmic unfolding of the seasons seen at their deepest level. This is how Steiner described it:

> I have tried to draw up verses for meditation, the effect of which will enable the soul gradually to discover in itself and in its own experiences the connection with the great cosmic constellations. These formulae for meditation do in all reality lead the soul out of its narrow confines to experience of the heavens. These fifty-two verses will enable the soul to find access to happenings in the great universe, and thereby to experience the spirits working in the onward flow of time. But if you ponder on the texts of the verses in the Calendar, you will discern an element

---

[2] Karl König, *The Calendar of the Soul: A Commentary* (Karl König Archive) Paperback, Floris Books, 2011.

of timelessness, in rhythmic alternation; an element that is experienced inwardly by the human being, the laws of which run parallel to those of time in the outer world.[3]

Further, in the introduction to the second German edition of the calendar in 1918 Steiner had this to say: "The year has a life of its own, and the human soul can share in that life and become part of it. . . . You should take these weekly meditations quite particularly into your hearts, for they contain what can make the soul alive and what really corresponds to a living relationship of the soul forces to the forces of the macrocosm."[4]

The heart quality of the experience of the calendar is emphasized by Karl König as well:

> Each single verse of the Soul Calendar contains not only a spiritual content which can be grasped intellectually but a powerful and substantial emotion, a strong feeling that changes from week to week. It is more important to carry this feeling in its ever-changing form through the year, than to connect oneself with the intellectual content of the verses—though this is necessary to achieve that feeling. If this is achieved, both in the course of the year and with the passing of the days, one's awareness is expanded and can gradually become a consciousness that extends over weeks, months and a year; and the result of this is that the human soul is able to live in harmony with the earthly world and the spirit-world.[5]

Something rather uncharacteristic may cause surprise when we take a closer look at the calendar's history. The calendar was formed of two parts: an extended Calendar of the Year, and a Calendar of the Soul that occupied only a small part of the publication.

The Calendar of the Year began on the first of April. The Calendar of the Soul started on Easter Sunday, in the week from April 7 to 13,

---

[3] Rudolf Steiner, *The Calendar of the Soul*, lecture of May 7, 1912.
[4] Quoted in Rudolf Steiner, *The Calendar of the Soul*, Daisy Aldan translator.
[5] Karl König, *The Calendar of the Soul: A Commentary*, 80–81.

1912. The shift from January to April was made in honor of the idea that the inauguration of our era should be tied to the year 33 AD of the Resurrection, the birth of the Christ-Being; not the year 1 of the birth of Jesus. The date of 33 AD as the birth of the "I" is crucial, because it reveals an important relationship between microcosm and macrocosm, in which Easter plays a central role. That was the time in which the human being awoke to the possibility of saying "I" to himself because the Christ had united with the Earth. Apparently the publication of the Calendar was the first time Steiner referred to the Mystery of Golgotha as the birth of the "I." This is why on the cover the characters "J C H" (Jesus Christ) appear, which also stand for the German *Ich*; and below appears the inscription *Geburt* (born). The whole reads "The year 1879 after the birth of the 'I.'" In effect, the year 1912 equals 1879, year of the inauguration of the Michael Age, plus thirty-three. Steiner wrote this at a time in which he could not yet speak openly of the Archangel Michael.

The preface to the first calendar was entitled "What Is Intended," and it was followed by a weekly calendar with drawings of the zodiac signs, which Imma von Eckhardstein had executed, following Steiner's sketches. These new signs were not meant to represent zodiacal constellations, but rather the "spiritual forces active in the cosmos." In addition to the twelve zodiacal images, also included were five images appearing at different times of the year, representing the five great epochs of Earth evolution (from Old Saturn to the present); a lunar calendar following the ephemeris; a daily calendar with commemoration of historical memorial days of great individualities, and only at the end, the Calendar of the Soul itself. Among the individualities commemorated in the days are Christian saints; biblical individuals (Enoch, Gaspar, Melchior, Balthasar, Abel, Seth, etc.); historical figures (Byron, Lessing, Galileo, Michelangelo, artists, philosophers, thinkers, and so forth). More curiously, individuals of stature whom Steiner did not exalt (for example, Roger Bacon and Charles Darwin) were also listed.

The first calendar was met, in Steiner's words, with "mockery and derision." The major unease lay in the fact that the year would have been variable and of unequal length. To that objection, Steiner responded that for anthroposophists, and only among themselves, it would be important to observe the year from Easter to Easter. He commented in a lecture specifically about the calendar, "In what is unequal there is life; in what is uniform and fixed, here is the impress of death."[6]

The Structure of the Calendar

In the natural scientific view, nature awakens at spring and falls asleep in the fall. Esoterically, the reverse is true: nature awakens in the fall and falls asleep in spring. And the human being follows this movement. This rhythm of the year is central to everything that is said afterward. It forms the foundation for the movement from thinking to "boding" that we will explore.

There is a double set of polarities in the Calendar. The first polarity divides the Calendar into two parts of the year, one going from Easter to Michaelmas, the other from Michaelmas to Easter. The second polarity divides the year through the Christmas/St. John's Tide axis.

This division of the calendar forms four quadrants of thirteen weeks. Nevertheless, seen more closely, the calendar is irregular from year to year, because of the position of Easter at its start. Given the cross structure of the calendar, for each verse in one quadrant of the Calendar there are three corresponding verses on the remaining quadrants, though not in a way that can be charted from mere logic. Every verse will be better understood in relation to the other three verses.

If we take the direction from spring to winter, the calendar starts at 1 at the lemniscate intersection of the equinoxes and culminates at 13 close to the Summer Solstice, returns from 13 to 1 at the intersection of the Fall Equinox, goes from 1 to 13 in the fall up to the time of Christmas and the Holy Nights, and returns from 13 to 1 during early spring at the time of Easter. Thus all verses numbered 1 are found close to the times of the equinoxes and all verses numbered 13 close to the solstices. The dynamic structure of the calendar appears most clearly in the lemniscate form, rather than in a circle.

In using the form of the lemniscate we are describing concentric circles moving from the center in four directions. The verses of cross 1 (or quartet 1) form the smallest circle at the center (equinox); the verses of cross 13 the

---

[6] Rudolf Steiner, *The Calendar of the Soul*, lecture of May 7, 1912.

largest one at the highest extension (solstice), and from the center to the periphery are placed another 11 crosses. To verse 1 of Easter correspond the following verses: verse 52 of the Holy Week, verse 26 of Michaelmas, and verse 27 of the week following Michaelmas.

To take another significant cross in terms of festivals let us look at cross 12. To St. John correspond verse 38 of Christmas, 40 of Epiphany, and verse 15 of approximately July 14–20.

Each verse has a complementary verse; they often appear side by side in various versions of the calendar. This is the verse that appears symmetrically through the equinoxes intersection on the other side of the year. If a verse is in the spring, its complement will be in the fall or winter. If a verse is in the summer, its complement will also be in the fall or winter. Verse 1 is linked to verse 52, verse 2 to 51, 3 to 50, and so on. These are the "counterparts" or "complementary verses."

There are another two ways in which verses are linked to each other. We have called *complementary* the verses linked through the equinox axis. We will call *mirror* verses those that correspond to each other across the solstice axes. This means that to each verse of the upper half of the lemniscate corresponds a mirror one in the upper half. The same is true of the lower half. To the Easter verse (1) corresponds the mirror verse 26 of Michaelmas; both are in the upper part of the lemniscate. To the Whitsun verse 8 corresponds the verse 19 on the opposite side of the lemniscate, it too a verse of cross 8. To the St. John verse (12) corresponds verse 15 (Figure 1).

The last way in which each verse is linked is a separation of 26 weeks, placing the other verse at the exact opposite time of the year. We will call this the *opposite* verse and will find it in the opposite loop of the lemniscate. To verse 1 of Easter is linked verse 27 of just after Michaelmas. To verse 8 of Whitsun corresponds verse 34 (November 24–30); to verse 12 of St. John, verse 38 of Christmas. The opposite verse is in fact the mirror verse of the complementary verse. An example: cross 1. Verse 1 of Easter has a complementary verse in 52, the verse of the Holy Week, and a mirror verse in 26, the time of Michaelmas. The complementary verse of 26 is 27, which is the opposite of verse 1.

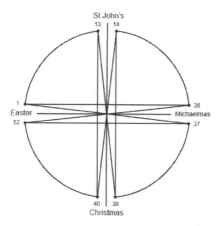

Figure 1: The Two Axes of the Calendar of the Soul

To summarize, we find the complementary and opposite verses of any given verse in opposing sides of the lemniscate; mirror verses in the same side of the lemniscate. The four verses each occupy four distinct quadrants.

Relating each verse to its complementary, mirror, and opposite verses forms a "quartet." Verse 1 forms a quartet with its complementary 52, its opposite 27, and mirror verse 26. Thus we have thirteen quartets dividing the year of 52 weeks. The sequences are 1/26/27/52 (quartet/cross 1); 2/25/28/51 (quartet/cross 2); 3/24/28/50, and so on.

With time in working with the Calendar of the Soul one can experience that what is set in motion with one verse of a quartet in late winter or early spring is carried further in the corresponding verses of the other quadrants. König equates the quadrants to beings of a higher order, that together "form the whole etheric or temporal structure of the year." And further: "Each of these time beings has its own face, its own character and even its own name. In the calendar König indicates time becomes space and "space is penetrated by the most wonderful lines of power."[7]

The Seasons' and Mid-Seasons' Quadrants

Let us return to the quadrants. These are spring from 1 to 13, summer from 14 to 26, fall from 27 to 38, winter from 39 to 52. They divide

<hr>

[7] Karl König, *The Calendar of the Soul: A Commentary*, 51-52.

the years in the intervals going roughly, but not exactly, from Easter to St. John, from St. John to Michaelmas, from Michaelmas to Christmas, from Christmas to Easter. The difference lies in the discrepancy between the Spring Equinox and Easter, which goes from a few days to 5 weeks, or on average 3 weeks each year. The summer apex of the lemniscate occurs between 2 and 3 weeks after St. John (verses 13 and 14), the fall intersection at the center between Michaelmas and the following week (verses 26 and 27), the winter apex of the lemniscate between the time of the Holy Nights and the week of Epiphany (verses 39 and 40), and the Spring Equinox intersection of the lemniscate at Easter between 1 to 5 weeks after the equinox. Thus the Calendar is closely allied to the rhythms of nature, but also slightly independent from them. And the human soul follows the movements of nature but also develops inner faculties that do not just mirror the natural tendency set by the season. Spiritual man is partly emancipated from natural man; still, the cycle of nature impresses definite changes in his soul.

Much of this work will look at the double division between the summer/winter pole of the calendar (intervals of 26 verses), to the season's quadrants: Easter to St. John, St. John to Michaelmas, Michaelmas to Christmas, Christmas to Easter. In addition the year of the Calendar can be subdivided in yet another set of quadrants, through the middle positions of each season's quadrants, or verses 7, 20, 33, and 46. These are the verses of so-called cross 7, which are the only ones of the year to divide the year in four equal sections. This division of the year will play an important role in the observance of the year through the Calendar in this work. The places in cross 7 mark strong warnings for a change in direction in the soul. König has called these "threshold" or "abyss verses" in which the soul faces temptations from the adversaries (Figure 2).

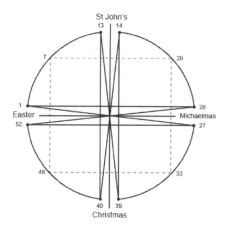

Figure 2: Square of Cross 7 in Relation to the
Two Axes of the Calendar of the Soul

Chapters 1 and 2 are built around the two halves of the year. Chapter 1 explores the in-breathing and out-breathing of the four ethers of the earth in the course of the year. Chapter 2 continues the exploration of the polarity thinking/boding that is part of König's work on the Calendar of the Soul.

Chapter 3 is central to all subsequent chapters. It introduces and explores the realms of cosmic life, cosmic light and cosmic warmth. We could say that these three cosmic realms and their metamorphoses in the human being are central to the whole work. The chapter also introduces the mid-season quadrants, defined by the verses of cross 7 and centered around equinoxes and solstices.

Chapters 4 to 6 explore the various themes that emerge around solstices and equinoxes, and reconnects these to the importance of cross 7. The whole is brought to a synthesis in chapter 7.

The various appendices explore some related themes (Appendices 1 to 3) and some unrelated ones (Appendices 4 to 6). Appendix 1 shows the flow between verses that allow those of you who feel fairly new to the experience of the calendar to detect themes and threads between following verses. Appendix 2 explores the structure of the calendar in relation to solstices and equinoxes on one hand, the season's quadrants and the Christian festivals on the other. In Appendix 3 we will survey the particular qualities of the mid-season's quadrants verses in a way that complements the rest of the work.

Appendix 4 explores the months' virtues in relation to the corresponding verses of the month. It draws upon the work of Herbert Witzenmann. Appendix 5 is a tentative exploration—one could say working notes—on the nature of the thirteen crosses/quartets of verses of the calendar. And finally, Appendix 6 revisits the structure of the calendar—in particular its division in the two parts of the year—in relation to the three practices outlined in the Foundation Stone Meditation.

CHAPTER 1

~~~~~~ 🌀 ~~~~~~

THE RHYTHM OF THE YEAR: IN-BREATHING AND OUT-BREATHING

In an Advent Address (47) König indicates, "The Calendar of the Soul is written out of the sphere of the spiritual course of time itself, where dwell those beings whom Rudolf Steiner calls the Spirits of the Cycles of Time."[8] This echoes what Steiner said of "the spirits working in the onward flow of time" in his lecture of May 7, 1912. This theme will occupy the present study, and we will peel its layers progressively. First we will explore what we could call a spiritual geography, an understanding of the deeper being of Gaia/Earth.

The Yearly Rhythms of the Earth and Their Relation to the Ethers

Immediately beyond the physical earth stands the etheric body of the Earth in which we find its elementals, and enveloping it further the Earth's astral body, where we find the Spirits of the Cycles of Time, the beings of the First Hierarchy—Seraphim, Cherubim, and Thrones.

To better follow the Earth in relation to the working of the Spirits of the Cycles of Time, we will look at how the formative forces work through the so-called ethers and to the yearly breathing cycle of the Earth. The four

---

[8] Rudolf Steiner, *The Calendar of the Soul*, lecture of May 7, 1912.

ethers are the link between spiritual beings and phenomenal manifestation; they link what stands beyond space to what manifests in space.

To each ether corresponds closer to the realm of manifestation one of the four elements. Ethers and elements complement each other; the elements are the terrestrial counterpart of the ethers.

In the evolution of Earth through its previous embodiments the ethers and elements have differentiated thus:

- In Old Saturn: birth of warmth ether and warmth (fire): in practice warmth and fire are one and the same.
- At the Old Sun stage, the light ether separated from the element of air.
- In Old Moon the chemical or tone ether separated from the element of water.
- During the present Earth stage, the life ether separated from the element of earth.

The ethers originate from the periphery of the cosmos and penetrate the human being in the formation of her etheric body. Ernst Marti, who has studied the question of the ethers in depth, concludes: "When the astral forces stream in by way of the portal of the stars (or streamed in during creation), they stimulate the ethers and create from them the formative forces. The spiritual forces penetrate more deeply into the elements and create in them the substances."[9]

Warmth is nonspatial and is the only element that dies away; it brings things into existence, helps them transform, and dies away. Fire and warmth exist as time, which originated in Old Saturn. They are not separated since there was no space as yet in Old Saturn; it only began in the successive Earth incarnation of Old Sun.

Light is essential for the appearance of space. It is through it that appear borders and distances. When we see the sun at dawn, things become visible and the space widens. As light separates in space, an inside from an outside, so air connects and fills the space. Air has no direction and structure, whereas light propagates in a linear fashion. The air can

---

[9] Ernst Marti, *The Four Ethers: Contributions to Rudolf Steiner's Science of the Ethers; Elements, Ethers, Formative Forces.*

be compressed, and it exerts pressure over the earth, whereas light has a suctional effect, carrying the gaze toward the periphery. The light ether is active as a centripetal force that pulls away from earth.

The tone or chemical ether finds its earthly reflection in the form of tones and music. Music is only possible through what divides and separates: intervals, distances, what appears simultaneously or in sequence. By contrast water always reconstitutes a whole; in a body of water the droplets merge. Water joins together and surrenders. In nature the action of the tone ether is visible in the division of trunk, branches, and twigs; in the nodes of the stem, standing in numerical relationship to each other. In water things grow together; through the tone ether they separate while still relating to each other.

The audible music becomes inner music in chemical relationships. We know that regular intervals interrelate chemical elements in the Mendeleev periodical table. Substances relate to and combine with each other according to laws of measure and number. The tone ether was known in the Mysteries of old as the "harmony of the spheres," and *harmonia* is that which arranges, creates order.

Whereas dense water has heaviness, the tone ether overcomes gravity. Thus the primary polarity of weight and levity is reflected in water/tone ether.

Earth and the life ether form the last polarity. On Earth we find for the first time in evolution the solid state, which brings fixity and immobility. The life ether animates what is solid and fixed; it gives it inner mobility. The earth element rejects since it separates at its surface; the life ether absorbs, it creates a skin that relates the inner to the outer and creates a whole. It gives form to space and differentiates the whole in the directions of space. An inanimate object, a rock is non-distinct: it has arbitrary boundaries that can be endlessly altered. The life ether creates living bodies and orients them through space. It enlivens and individualizes, organizes as a unity.

In Old Saturn space did not exist; it was not possible to speak of dimensions of space. Thus fire and warmth are not separated and are practically the same.

Air and light express themselves in one dimension: light in the linearity of its rays, air in its tension and elasticity. The plant lives within this dimension, in the polarity of earth and sun. It manifests in radial symmetry, except when astrality penetrates more deeply and expresses an animal element in the flower; this introduces bilateral symmetry, rather than radial symmetry, as in the example of leguminous flowers.

Water forms planes everywhere; it flows in laminar planes moving over each other. The plane dimension is mirrored in the element of symmetry that forms pairs of tones or nodes in the plants. It is through water and tone that arises the development of the embryo, which on one hand grows two elements together and on the other separates and differentiates. Tone and water allow for the development of two dimensions that we see in animal life; only two since the animal knows right and left, front and back, but does not yet have the erect position and therefore no up and down. Here, as already mentioned, appears bilateral symmetry.

Through earth and the life ether the three dimensions appear. An inanimate object has no true center; this appears in the living through the nucleus or the heart. The three dimensionality appears in the human being thanks to the upright position, which gives us individuality.

The Breathing of the Ethers

Something else appears in the ethers when we go from the oldest (warmth ether) through the most recent (life ether). The later ethers, more evolved, contain the attributes of the older ones. The light ether includes the warmth ether; the life ether encompasses all the ethers. Another important differentiation occurs between the two older and the two younger ethers:

- Warmth and light ethers act centrifugally, toward the cosmos; they are radiating, expansive, and act in the gaseous atmosphere of the earth.
- Chemical and life ethers act centripetally toward the earth; they have concentrating, suctional forces and act on the liquid, solid masses of earth.

The Earth organism tends to bring about a situation of static equilibrium of four concentric circles. In this situation no life nor evolution would be possible. The forces of the cosmos disturb this equilibrium and the order of the layers, causing weather phenomena, the seasons, and the possibility of life on Earth with all its variations.

In the daily rhythm of the Earth the centripetal forces, more particularly the chemical ether, is exhaled in the morning into the light ether; it is inhaled and brought back toward the earth in the evening. Around sunrise and sunset we have maximum barometric pressure in the lower atmosphere and maximum humidity in the soil (Figure 3).

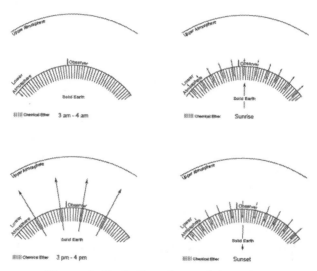

Figure 3: Daily Breathing of the Ethers

To the maximums at sunrise and sunset correspond minimums toward 3–4 a.m. and 3–4 p.m., which are reflected in the barometric pressure and humidity. At 3–4 p.m. we have minimum barometric pressure and much higher humidity in the whole atmosphere in relation to the earth. At 3–4 a.m. we have minimum barometric pressure and much lower humidity in the whole atmosphere.

In the seasonal rhythm occurs a larger exhaling and inhaling of the chemical ether into the light and warmth ethers. Exhalation occurs at the beginning of the spring, and water starts to rise in plants and trees. It reaches its apex at the height of summer with the culmination of plant growth. The chemical ether is then gradually inhaled back in the fall and reaches its highest contraction at the time of winter. Water starts to descend in the plants and the formative forces penetrate the body of the earth (Figure 4).

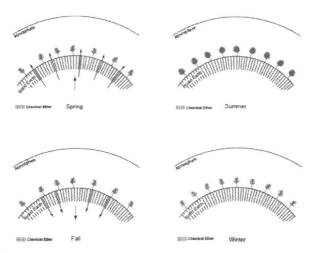

Figure 4: Yearly Breathing of the Ethers

The understanding of the above, external cycle of the year, is deepened when we look at the beings that accompany it.

The In-Breathing and Out-Breathing of the Earth

Guenther Wachsmuth has led us through the in-breathing and out-breathing of the Earth during the year from the perspective of nature. The picture can be enlarged if we include the work of spiritual beings in the whole picture. We will turn mostly to what Steiner has offered us in *The Cycle of the Year as Breathing Process of the Earth*.[10] This view will be enlarged in the chapters that treat of solstices and equinoxes.

At Winter Solstice the Earth is holding her forces, her soul element, within; it can be compared to the human being holding his breath within. In a sense we could say it is not speaking to the heavens. This is the time in which the birth of Jesus happened.

At the Spring Equinox the earth breathes out and the soul is still half within the Earth. The Earth-soul, permeated with the Christ element,

---

[10] Rudolf Steiner, *The Cycle of the Year as Breathing Process of the Earth*, lectures of March 31 and April 4, 1923.

pours out into the spiritually permeated cosmic space. The Christ forces coming from the Earth start to work with Sun forces around Easter. Christ rises into the cosmos accompanied by Michael, who seeks to renew the forces he uses up in fall and winter.

At St. John the Earth has completely exhaled, pouring out its soul-element into the cosmos and taking into itself the forces of Sun and stars. These forces are reflected on the surface of the Earth, for example in the forms of the flowers. We are moved to living with the cosmos rather than just with the Earth. "What appears in world space springing and sprouting from the Earth in thousandfold colors—this is of the same nature. Only it is a reflection, a raying-back force, whereas we bear in our human souls the original force itself."[11] The earth becomes a mirror of the cosmos in the summer. Since the Christ impulse is taken into the Earth's exhaled breath, foregoing the Earth, this one is overtaken by Ahrimanic forces, which the human being will find upon its return in the fall.

At Michaelmas the Earth starts to inhale. We take back within ourselves everything we have received from the cosmos through the Christ impulse. Michael comes to meet humanity and has to overcome the Ahrimanic dragon. In uniting himself with the Earth's in-breathing, Michael prepares the way for Christ Jesus.

At Christmas time, because Michael has purified the Earth, the Christ impulse lives in the earth itself. In the cycle of the year we see Michael preparing the way for the Christ, at different points in time contending with powers at work on Earth and in the cosmos.

The yearly breathing cycle of the Earth leads to the distinction between the spring/summer time of the year and the fall/winter time. During the warm part of the year we could say that human being experiences an expanded nature consciousness and during the cold part of the year a contracted self-consciousness.[12]

---

[11] *The Cycle of the Year as Breathing Process of the Earth*, lecture of March 31, 1923.
[12] These are the terms used by Steiner in the lecture *The Michael Imagination* of October 5, 1923.

CHAPTER 2

SUMMER AND WINTER:
INTUITION AND THINKING

The first obvious division that appears in the calendar is that of the warm and cold seasons, the upper and lower parts of the lemniscate. These correspond respectively to the out-breathing and in-breathing of the Earth organism, the exhaling of the tone/chemical ether into the light and warmth ethers, and the inhaling back into the earth. During the spring and summer the Earth and the human being reach out to the cosmos; during the winter the Earth is at its most contracted state. In this yearly rhythm we are received in the bosom of the hierarchies; they offer gifts from the cosmos in the summer, which we work to integrate in the winter when we are most contracted within our souls. This has brought some to equate the two halves of the year to what Owen Barfield calls "original participation" in the summer and "conscious participation" in the winter.

Conscious participation corresponds to self-consciousness. Original participation has a wider connotation since it is an evolutionary expression. Humanity was most fully part of original participation when it possessed atavistic clairvoyance. At present only part of this finds its expression in the spring-summer part of the year; the human being, who has grown out of atavistic clairvoyance, enters in spring and summer a state of soul that is reminiscent of it. Nature consciousness, however, only means receptivity to the forces of the cosmos, not a losing of self in these forces, as we will see below.

The Calendar of the Soul reflects our journey through the ethers during the year. The expressions *cosmic life, cosmic light,* and *cosmic warmth* reflect this reality, though they also encompass something larger and lead us to the realms of the cosmic Word and of cosmic thinking.

The terms *cosmic life* and many related ones appear both in the early spring and in early fall at the times when the out-breathing or in-breathing just begins. After somewhere between verses 4 and 7 we hear more and more about cosmic light, and this theme is woven with cosmic warmth from around Whitsun to the time of St. John. The human being rises toward the divine and has to develop to consciously receive what the spiritual world wants to bestow.

In descending toward fall, the Calendar follows the theme of the fading of warmth and light. Cold and darkness are announced around Michaelmas and after. The themes of life, light, and warmth appear then metamorphosed in the human being since external life, light, and warmth steadily diminish when the world is covered in darkness and cold. It is the human being who is now called to create them out of conscious spiritual striving.

We will now look at the two halves of the year. We have called them the times of nature-consciousness and self-consciousness. In Karl König's work this division of the year is reflected in the contrast between two main soul-faculties: boding (spring and summer) and thinking (fall and winter), which will occupy most of the considerations of this chapter.

In order to offer a brief sketch of the succession of the themes through the seasons and to sense the threads that unite verse to verse, we refer the reader to Appendix 1.

Boding/Intuition

The following are reflections about the attitude of soul that guides us best through the spring and summer months, when the soul of the Earth breathes out toward the cosmos and the human being tends to follow this movement at the risk of losing herself in external sense impressions and stimulations. Boding/intuition then offers an inner compass.

The word *Ahnung* ("boding" is the translation in English that König used) is of Central European origin and first appeared in Middle High German in the form of the verb *ahnen* toward the end of the 11th century. Since the beginning it meant "to have a dark premonition."

The new word emerged before the turning point of European consciousness in which Europe saw the birth of Scholasticism as the refinement of the flower of thinking. Close in time the year 1250 marked the point in which even the highest initiates could not carry in their consciousness anything other than faint memories of their initiations. This is also why the modern paths of initiation took their start soon after; in this we think of Rosicrucianism most of all.

In boding we can experience a mood mixed with anxiety and fear. Boding invites an awareness of conditions and circumstances not clearly apprehended. This can either be completely misleading or bring intuitively apprehended objective realities into consciousness. Boding is what offers us inklings and insights for the way ahead.

When it comes to characterizing boding, one has to go by exclusion: it is neither conscious nor unconscious, nor can it be compared to dreaming. It works as foreknowledge, as a kind of preconsciousness; in the best case scenario, it is something revealed that will later turn out to be true.

It is because the senses overpower our thinking that we need recourse to boding. By extension this applies when something that must be decided cannot just be fully apprehended from sensory input alone; cannot just be thought out. Boding can be seen as the soul's dialogue with cosmic creative thoughts at the time of the year in which they cannot be apprehended from a distance, but can only be "lived in."

In the German *ahnung* we find articulated a compound of ideas. Boding, König offers, can be defined as "an awareness of conditions and circumstances that are not clearly apprehended."[13] Overall, it is a state of gestation that acquires strength until it can be known and expressed with certainty. Boding is what directs us toward an understanding of events in our lives and an awakening to their deeper meaning.

---

[13] Karl König, *The Calendar of the Soul: A Commentary*, 195.

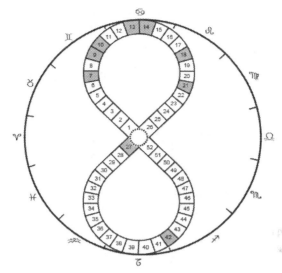

Figure 5: Verses that Refer to Boding/Intuition

Other words that can express this reality of the soul are used in various translations of the Calendar of the Soul: *intimation, divining* or *heart's divining, expectation, inner voice, presentiment, intuition, awareness stirring in the heart, feeling dimly hinting, inner prompting*.[14] In more than one way, boding corresponds to the modern sense of the word *intuition* (to be distinguished from true Intuition, which follows Imagination and Inspiration), and I like to add *heart sensing*, an expression I have heard from Coen van Houten. In this essay I will from now on refer to intuition. Figure 5 offers reference to the verses in which the word *ahnung* and its derivatives appear in the Calendar of the Soul.

Intuition is ushered in by feeling in verses 3 and 4. In verse 3 mindfulness of our primal state is something that the soul can feel rather than know. The same is true for sounding the depth(s) of our true being. In verse 4 feeling comes to the fore as "perceptive feeling."

The word *ahnung* appears nine times in the calendar; seven occur in the half of the year from Easter to Michaelmas. From now on we will use the terms present in Hans Pusch's translation of the Calendar and place in brackets the translations used by Cecil Harwood, in which the word

---

[14] Rudolf Steiner, *The Calendar of the Soul by Rudolf Steiner with Translations by Daisy Aldan, John F. Gardner, Isabel Grieve, Brigitte Knaack, Ernst Lehrs and Ruth and Hans Pusch and a Paraphrase by Owen Barfield.*

ahnung and its compound forms are systematically translated as "boding." What function boding plays can be fully understood in verse 7, in which it first appears, just as spring comes into full expression, after the time of ascension. The air pulsates with life and the human being can apprehend the nature of the etheric:

> My self is threatening to fly forth,
> Lured strongly by the world's enticing light.
> Come forth now, prophetic feeling [boding],
> Take up with strength your rightful task:
> Replace in me the power of thought
> Which in the senses' glory
> Would ever lose itself.

This statement indicates that during half of the year intuition has a place equal to that of thinking in fall and winter. We fully enter now the time of the year in which we develop a sort of nature-consciousness, a new stage of the atavistic consciousness that experienced itself in communion with the worlds of spirit but knew no self-consciousness. Intuition wrests us from losing ourselves in the senses and the light. Though we enter a state of dreaming, we can now wrest from it inklings and insights of things to be. Two weeks later, just after Whitsun, we are told:

> When I forget the narrow will of self,
> The cosmic warmth that heralds summer's glory
> Fills all my soul and spirit;
> To lose myself in light
> Is the command of spirit-vision
> And intuition [prophetic boding] tells me strongly:
> O lose yourself to find yourself.

Here is a key distinction between the roles of thinking and boding/intuition, as König emphasizes. Thinking can point to the reality of dying and becoming, but it becomes experience in intuition. Through intuition higher insights are brought to birth than is possible through thinking alone at this time of the year. Then in verse 10 intuition appears again as presentiment:

To summer's radiant heights
The sun in shining majesty ascends;
It takes my human feeling
Into its own wide realms of space.
Within my inner being stirs
Presentiment [prophetic boding] which heralds dimly;
You shall in future know:
A godly being now has touched you.

This verse amplifies the complementary roles of intuition and thinking. Intuition paves the way for what thinking cannot apprehend in the heights of summer. At the other end of the year, what intuition feels and experiences can be brought to clear consciousness through the light of thinking.

In verse 13, just after St. John's Tide, when the soul reaches to the heights of the impetus to excarnate, we are told:

And when I live in senses' heights,
There flames up deep within my soul
Out of the spirit's fiery worlds
The gods' own word of truth:
In spirit sources seek expectantly [seek through your boding power]
To find your spirit kinship.

This verse constitutes a turning point, as becomes clear in verses 14 and 15. The process of dying and becoming that was announced at Whitsun is completed at this point. In nature take place the first processes of decay. In verse 14 (July 7 to 13) we read:

Surrendering to senses' revelation
I lost the drive of my own being,
And dreamlike thinking seemed
To daze and rob me of my self.
Yet quickening there draws near
In sense appearance cosmic thinking.

If he has expanded his being in all that grows, blossoms, and fruits in devotion and warmth of soul toward the universe, the human being enters a silent relationship with the hierarchies and has an intimation of their speech. The next verse, 15, is an encouragement to hold within, nurture, and preserve the cosmic thinking and spirit brotherhood that the "I" cannot comprehend in the light of thinking at the height of summer. The reason for, and gesture of, intuition becomes manifest in this verse:

I feel enchanted weaving
Of spirit within outer glory.
In dullness of the senses
It has enwrapt my being
In order to bestow the strength
Which in its narrow bounds my I
Is powerless to give itself.

This powerlessness of the conscious self is the reason for the protective and nurturing role of intuition during the summer. In verse 18 we read:

Can I expand my soul
That it unites itself
With cosmic Word received as seed?
I sense [I do forebode] that I must find the strength
To fashion worthily my soul
As fitting raiment for the spirit.

By tending to the field of the soul we create the ground in which the gifts of the spirit may start to grow. With the end of summer, intuition acquires more strength and moves us outward with a deeper certainty of self. König points to intuition having been initially given to us from outside ourselves, whereas now it has rooted inwardly. It is starting to complete its path. Verse 21 reads:

I feel strange power, bearing fruit
And gaining strength to give myself to me.
I sense the seed maturing

And expectation [boding power], light-filled, weaving
Within me on my selfhood's power.

Here boding is presented with an assertive "selfhood's power." Through this further step, we gain assurance that the seeds planted in the soul in summer will reach maturation in the winter.

Now we come to the two other mentions of boding in the fall-winter part of the year. Immediately after Michaelmas, we hear in verse 27: "To dive into my being's depths stirs up a yearning in me, boding well . . ."

When to my being's depths I penetrate,
There stirs expectant longing [yearning in me, boding well]
That self-observing, I may find myself
As gift of summer sun, a seed
That warming lives in autumn mood
As germinating force of soul.

At this stage intuition is no longer tentative; it has a quality of confirmation. Looking at the fading of light and warmth in external nature, intuition knows it is coming to the end of its role; it has brought the sun deep within the soul, Intuition, appearing for the last time, passes the baton to thinking, which appears with power in the following verse with an assertive "radiance of my thought." Then the word does not reemerge until the end of January. In verse 42 intuition has a forward-looking gesture and is associated with an intimation of the coming sense-world's revelation. This is the verse that announces the dawn of boding, just as verse 27 announces its sunset:

In this the shrouding gloom of winter
The soul feels ardently impelled
To manifest its innate strength,
To guide itself to realms of darkness,
Anticipating thus [feeling in new forebodement]
Through warmth of heart the sense-world's revelation.

Intuition works hand in hand with what we can call conscience. König reaches the conclusion that it "directs man's attention to the guidance

15

of his destiny" and that "the dawning light of karma works within as boding."[15]

Thinking

When we look at the fall/winter time of the year (verses 27 to 52) we can clearly recognize that an inner stance is required of the human being: the development of clear thinking.

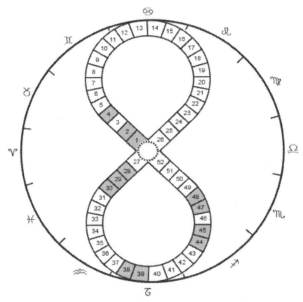

Figure 6: Verses that Refer to Thinking

The world creative thoughts of the summer have been received in the soul opened through soul warmth and devotion. The heritage of summer creates in the soul a yearning for redeeming and continuing the work of creation, through that human consciousness which alone can reflect creation to itself. In a strengthened self it is thinking that can achieve its goal in a patient work of refinement and ennoblement that will take the whole of the winter arc of the year. Figure 6 offers reference to the verses in which thinking appears in the Calendar of the Soul.

---

[15] Karl König, *The Calendar of the Soul: A Commentary*, 204.

The ground has been prepared through the summer and has come to a culmination in verses 25 to 27 that affirm unequivocally the birth of the self: "I can belong now to myself" (25), "that sense of self spring forth from it [from the will]" (26), and "find myself self contemplating" (27). This affirmation of self precedes the first mention of thinking in "*radiance* of my thought" coming from soul's *sun* power (28):

> I can, in newly quickened inner life,
> Sense wide horizons in my self.
> The force and radiance of my thought—
> Coming from soul's sun power—
> Can solve the mysteries of life,
> And grant fulfilment now to wishes
> Whose wings have long been lamed by hope.

The human being has received the light of divine creative thoughts in the summer. Thinking appears as that force which maintains and creates the "soul's Sun power," a force that can develop insights and offer concrete, immediate hope. This power will in fact create the "summer of the soul" that is announced in verse 30. Intuition has carried and nurtured the power of the sun inwardly; it has allowed the sun's power to shine on the seed of the self. Now that the outer sun has retreated, thinking floods the soul as an inner sun and strives to radiate outwardly.

Soon after the first mention of thinking, the soul is asked to "fan the spark of thinking into flame" (29):

> To fan the spark of thinking into flame
> By my own strong endeavor,
> To read life's inner meaning
> Out of the cosmic spirit's fount of strength:
> This is my summer heritage,
> My autumn solace, and my winter hope.

Verse 29 deserves a mention of its own because it is the fulcrum of the passage from summer to winter and from intuition to thinking. Intuition is echoed in the mention of "read life's inner meaning out of the cosmic spirit fount of strength." Intuition and thinking are further integrated through mention of "summer heritage and winter hope." The Michaelic trust in the wise world guidance of the spirit resounds in this verse. All these qualities are continued and made more explicit in verse 30:

> There thrive within the sunlight of my soul
> The ripened fruits of thinking;
> To conscious self-assurance
> The flow of feeling is transformed.
> I can perceive now joyfully
> The autumn's spirit-waking:
> The winter will arouse in me
> The summer of the soul.

Feeling emerges from the realm of the dream with steady assurance, in supporting a thinking power that becomes summer of the soul. In verse 31 it is not thinking but light that strives outward sun-imbued from spirit depths. And in verse 32 thinking is not mentioned, but its results "clearer insight" into the weaving of life's destiny.

While thinking is not mentioned in verses 34 to 36, in parallel to verses 25 to 27 it is the self that continues to grow: "new risen sense of self" (34), "my Self as humble part within the cosmic Self" (35). In verse 37 thinking is not mentioned but rather "spirit light" in conjunction with Word Divine (cosmic Word).

Just as the cosmic Word entered the depth of our being through the threshold of the senses in summer, now this encounter is made conscious in the soul and is celebrated as the spirit-birth at the time of Christmas:

> The spirit child within my soul
> I feel freed of enchantment.
> In heart-high gladness has
> The holy cosmic Word engendered
> The heavenly fruit of hope,
> Which grows rejoicing into worlds afar
> Out of my being's godly roots.

The spirit child, fruit of the spirit-birth, is mentioned in 38 (Christmas) as the gift of cosmic Word. In verse 39 thinking is further intensified:

Surrendering to spirit revelation
I gain the light of cosmic being;
The power of thinking, growing clearer,
Gains strength to give myself to me,
And quickening there frees itself
From thinker's energy my sense of self.

Thinking permeated by the force of cosmic Word reveals to us who we truly are and is the instrument for receiving revelation. The two themes of the emerging of Self and the growing power of thinking meet and fructify each other now that we have met with cosmic Self and have reached the spirit-birth through the power of the cosmic Word striving to become conscious in our soul.

Now the cosmic Word present in our soul's core touches the realms of the heart to become capacity for love. Verse 40 mentions the "fiery power of the *cosmic Word*, filling the vain delusion of my Self." Verse 41 mentions the "heart's own core" and "human loving and human working." "Warmth of heart" is restated in verse 42. And in verse 43 this is amplified in terms of "glowing warmth," "forces of the heart," and "inner fire." Where thinking is not mentioned, it is the forces of the heart that come to the fore bringing a transformation. This is the preparation for the unfolding of love in verse 48.

In verse 44 a new quality is added to thinking:

In reaching for new sense attractions,
Soul-clarity would fill,
Mindful of spirit-birth attained,
The world's bewildering, sprouting growth
With the creative will of my own thinking.

Fall and winter have ushered in a strengthening of the will. Instead of surrendering to the cosmos as in the summer, the soul has been strengthening itself, while purifying the will, turning it into the Michaelic will announced in verse 26. With this purified will, thinking can now prepare itself for the return of the forces of life and light. The will in thinking is what outwardly manifests as growth, and now we prepare to recognize the kinship of these powers.

In verse 45 the previous clarity becomes "power of thought united with the spirit's birth" in conjunction with the meeting with the world of the senses:

> My power of thought grows firm
> United with the spirit's birth.
> It lifts the senses' dull attractions
> To bright-lit clarity.
> When soul-abundance
> Desires union with the world's becoming,
> Must senses' revelation
> Receive the light of thinking.

Thinking is revealed as that power which not only sheds light on the world's becoming, but also which intimately unites us with it. Furthermore it is that power which creation seeks for its fulfilment through the human being. Thinking enlivens the senses, and with it our participation in the world of nature is rendered conscious. The striving of this time of the year is rendered manifest in this verse and in the following ones.

The importance of the will is emphasized in 46 together with the threat of the world that could stunt the inborn forces of the soul. The soul has more to do in order to withstand the threat of the world of the senses to its inner forces. It is an effort of the will stimulated by the conscious memory of all that has been achieved through the dark time of the year.

Verse 47 is the epitome of strength and of the will in thinking: "strength of thought well armed by powers divine, which live with strength."

> There will arise out of the world's great womb
> Quickening the senses' life, the joy of growth.
> Now may it find my strength of thought
> Well armed by powers divine
> Which live with strength within my being.

This is thinking imbued through and through with the forces of the will. At a time in which the human being feels more and more united with nature and feels the coming of cosmic thoughts in the bursting forth of growth, "certainty of cosmic thinking" can awaken love (48):

> Within the light that out of world-wide heights
> Would stream with power toward the soul,
> May certainty of cosmic thinking
> Arise to solve the soul's enigma,
> And focusing its mighty rays,
> Awaken love within the hearts of man.

Here we find fulfilled the promise of verse 29 of uniting wisdom of thinking with strength coming from a cosmic spirit's fount. Fully spiritualized thinking is that force which redeems our Self and renders us a force for good for nature and our fellow human being. The self is no longer the power that divides us from nature and fellow human beings.

Cosmic thinking means concretely the union of the "force of cosmic life" and "clarity of thought" in 49, and in 50 this becomes "mighty revelation" from the powers of nature ("joy of growth") and union with these. This is what manifests as the power of spiritualized thinking. The coming of cosmic day of 49 is not just the awaiting of the outer expression of spring, but the rejoicing at the recurrence of Christ's resurrection from the grave of the spiritualized Earth.

The penetration into the realm of cosmic life and the deed of Golgotha at Easter now call us into another sphere of experience through the Christ fully drawing us into the paradisal experience of original participation, through the longing toward our original human experience, of that which we were and are truly meant to be. It is not just the human being that is longing for cosmic life; it is also the spirit world yearning to find its achievement through human self-consciousness.

Now the power of thinking reaches its goal. It forms a bridge but can no longer accompany us as is indicated quite appropriately in the Easter verse. Cosmic life, the permeation of our being through the higher ethers, receives a new impulse at Easter through that being Who comes from its realm:

When out of world-wide spaces
The sun speaks to the human mind,
And gladness from the depths of soul
Becomes, in seeing one with light,
Then rising from the sheath of self,
Thoughts soar to distances of space
And dimly bind
Man's being with the spirit's life.

Thinking unites with those forces from which it originates, the formative forces that shape on one hand the world of nature and on the other the thinking capacity in the human being. This creates a sense of felt but unconscious union ("dimly bind man's being to the spirit's life"). Human thinking quietly lays to rest; world formative forces, the thoughts of the cosmos, will bestow blessings on the human being. The human being can face the transformative permeation of the Earth through the realms of cosmic life, with gladness of soul.

The central insight of Karl König in relation to the complementary roles of thinking and boding plays down to the end in the spring and fall times of the year. Each passes the baton to the other like a gentleman. In the very early spring (verse 1) "thoughts soar to distances of space and dimly bind man's being to the spirit's life," the latter being an expression for cosmic life. In verse 2 "thinking loses self-confines," and in verse 7, at the threshold of the new mid-season quadrant, the power of thought "which in the senses' glory would ever lose itself" fades in order for intuition to "take up with strength your rightful task." Where one ends the other starts.

What happens at the other end of the year is equally instructive. In verse 21 intuition lovingly presides to the growth of selfhood's power. In verse 27 (opposite of 1) intuition looks forward with expectation to and surrounds with its light the Self living in the soul as "germinating force of soul." This is the last we hear of intuition, simply because in the next verse "the radiance of thought, coming from soul's sun power" majestically ushers in thinking as the rising sun on the horizon of the soul.

To round off this exploration we will first turn to the place of feeling in relation to intuition and thinking. We will then turn to those terms that appear at both ends of the year, but in diametrically polar ways: cosmic thinking and cosmic Word.

Feeling in Relation to Intuition/Boding and Thinking

At first sight, feeling would seem more associated to intuition. Though this association exists, in actual fact most of the mention of feeling words—*fühl* and its derivatives—occur in relation to thinking (4 for intuition, 8 for thinking) and to the period of thinking's ascendancy. In effect, as we will see feeling forms a bridge between the two soul faculties. Figure 7 offers reference to the verses in which the word *fühl* and its derivatives appear in the Calendar of the Soul and their relationship to the faculties of intuition/boding and thinking.

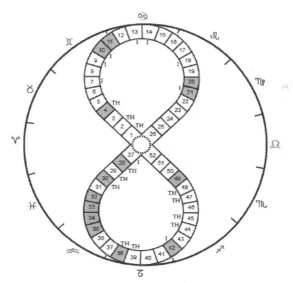

Figure 7: Verses in Which References to Feeling Appear, in Relation to Verses that Reference Thinking and Intuition

We will start our exploration from verse 4, situated 3 weeks after Easter. Thinking has started to wane on the horizon of the soul; in fact it plays a passive, recipient role in the verse. Feeling rises for the first time, and announces a future goal:

I sense [*fühle*] a kindred nature to my own:
Thus speaks perceptive feeling
As in the sun-illuminated world
It merges with the floods of light;
To thinking's clarity
And firmly bind as one
The human being and the world.

This verse of cross 4 announces the goal that will be reached in verses 30 and 49, all of them part of cross 4. We will return to these. Intuition rises to prominence as the main soul task in verses 7, 9, and 10. Feeling follows closely on 10 and 11. In 10 this appears as the following:

To summer's radiant heights
The sun in shining majesty ascends;
It takes my human feeling
Into its own wide realms of space.
Within my inner being stirs
Presentiment [intuition] which heralds dimly;
You shall in future know:
A godly being now has touched you.

It is from feeling that intuition takes the strength to recognize the godly being in future time. In the following verse, feeling supports what intuition asks the human I to accomplish, "lose itself and find itself in the cosmic I"

In this the sun's high hour it rests
With you to understand these words of wisdom:
Surrender to the beauty of the world,
Be stirred with new-enlivened feeling;
The human I can lose itself
And find itself within the cosmic I.

Devotion-filled feeling accompanies the soul's intuition of the need to trust losing itself in the cosmic I.

Feeling then only reappears toward the beginning of the Fall Equinox mid-season quadrant, in verses 20 and 21. Here too, it is closely associated with intuition in verses 18 and 21. Verse 20 is the warning verse in which the soul acquires a sense of its own place in relation to the macrocosm. It wants to awaken to the reality and fullness of selfhood's power, which bridges individual and world:

I feel at last my life's reality
Which, severed from the world's existence,
Would in itself obliterate itself
And building only on its own foundation
Would in itself bring death upon itself.

It is this selfhood's power that intuition wants to confirm and uphold in the following verse. It is the destination and goal of intuition in the summer. Its achievement comes in verse 21, where intuition is woven through and through with feeling:

I feel strange power, bearing fruit
And gaining strength to give myself to me.
I sense the seed maturing
And expectation, light-filled, weaving
Within me on my selfhood's power.

The next time in which intuition appears is in autumn, and it serves to confirm the goal of selfhood (verse 27):

When to my being's depths I penetrate,
When to my being's depths I penetrate,
There stirs expectant longing [intuition]
That self-observing, I may find myself
As gift of summer sun, a seed
That warming lives in autumn mood
As germinating force of soul.

Feeling now enters the fall-winter half of the year. Not surprisingly it makes its start where intuition leaves off and appears in conjunction with thinking, which is just starting to rise on the horizon of the soul:

I can, in newly quickened inner life,
Sense wide horizons in myself.
The force and radiance of my thought—
Coming from soul's Sun power—
Can solve the mysteries of life,
And grant fulfilment now to wishes
Whose wings have long been lamed by hope.

Just as feeling is amplified when intuition concludes its summer journey, so now feeling appears as a confirmation of the expansive power of thinking. Thinking is affirmed with all the attributes of the external sun, and it ushers in new promises for the arc of the winter of the soul. As a result the individual feels enlivened and strengthened with new confidence.

We now will witness a crescendo of six feeling-related verses, from 30 to 38, preceding the next mention of thinking's role in 39. Let us see this sequence. Verse 30, as announced earlier, belongs to cross 4. It brings the promise of 4 closer to realization:

There flourish within the sunlight of my soul
The ripened fruits of thinking;
To conscious self-assurance
The flow of feeling is transformed.
I can perceive now joyfully
The autumn's spirit-waking:
The winter will arouse in me
The summer of the soul.

The themes of assurance and expansion are here reinstated. The warmth of feeling now truly supports thinking and promises to transform the experience of winter into one of summer of the soul. The same promise of soul confidence is taken a step further in verse 32:

I feel my own force, bearing fruit
And gaining strength to give me to the world.
My inmost being I feel charged with power

To turn with clearer insight
Toward the weaving of life's destiny.

Feeling appears here twice, in conjunction with the related ideas of power, force, or strength. The human being is assured of her place in the world and in the fabric of her karmic relationships.

We now come to the new threshold verse (33), and what has been announced in the previous threshold verse (20) is reaffirmed. The world's reality, which we wanted to connect with in 20, has now become something that we can connect and contribute to via feeling:

I feel at last the world's reality
Which, lacking the communion of my soul,
Would by itself be frosty, empty life,
And showing itself powerless
To recreate itself in souls,
Would in itself find only death.

Through thinking, whose role has been ascending in the fall, the soul has gained assurance of its relationship with the macrocosm. It is feeling that first senses the coming task of humanity's co-creator role in the order of the cosmos. As to how this will begin to happen, the soul is feeling once more that leads the way in verse 34. It senses the living relationship between self and spirit self that is denoted with the expression "sense of Self." It is from this source that pour cosmic forces:

In secret inwardly to feel
How all that I've preserved of old
Is quickened by new-risen sense of self:
This shall, awakening, pour cosmic forces
Into the outer actions of my life
And growing, mould me into true existence.

The emergence of the sense of Self gives feeling the further assurance that it can seek itself and find itself within its macrocosmic counterpart, the cosmic Self, in verse 35.

Can I know life's reality
So that it's found again
Within my soul's creative urge?
I feel that I am granted power
To make my Self, as humble part,
At home within the cosmic Self.

Sense of Self and cosmic Self lead the soul to the experience of the spirit-birth at Christmas time (verse 38). A veil is torn, and the spirit child, fruit of the spirit-birth, is felt "free of enchantment" at the center of the soul. The strengthening of feeling from verses 30 to 38 ushers in the return of thinking, at a new level in close association to the "sense of self" in verse 39:

Surrendering to spirit revelation
I gain the light of cosmic being:
The power of thinking, growing clearer,
Gains strength to give myself to me,
And quickening there frees itself
From thinker's energy my sense of Self.

We witness here a next step in the growth of the power of thinking. Its last mention in verse 30 indicated its close alliance with the "flow of feeling" and the expansive feelings of joy and confidence in the future. This attains a new level of realization in verse 39, witness the expressions "light of cosmic being" and "sense of Self."

We are nearing the end of our explorations. In the wintertime feeling appears twice more. The first time it is not in relation to thinking, but rather to revelation (verse 42).

In this the shrouding gloom of winter
The soul feels ardently impelled
To manifest its innate strength,
To guide itself to realms of darkness,
Anticipating thus [feeling in new forebodement]
Through warmth of heart the sense-world's revelation.

Here, it is a feeling strengthened to the utmost that can confidently see the human being's role in affirming the world's existence. In the next verse it is in effect through forces of the heart that the human being can, not just anticipate, but "give the world of appearance the power to be."

The culmination of feeling's journey comes just at the time of Lent as the soul prepares for the Easter's resurrection of nature in verse 49. Here, as in the previous verses of cross 4 (4 and 30) feeling is closely allied to thinking. Here, in fact, thinking expresses itself through feeling:

I feel the force of cosmic life:
Thus speaks my clarity of thought,
Recalling its own spirit growth
Through nights of cosmic darkness,
And to the new approach of cosmic day
It turns its inward rays of hope.

When looked at more closely, we can now recognize in intuition/boding a manifestation of the will in the recognition of truth. Through boding the will seeks its place in the world at the time in which it would lose itself in the dream of summer. Intuition is the attempt to bring to realization through the will what cannot be clearly apprehended through the light of thinking. It is the will's striving to experience, rather than know, truth and witness the (re-)birth of the self within the microcosm of the soul. This is carried out through the calls expressed by the voices and the imperatives of the soul calling to action.

In wintertime strengthened thinking gives us a place and standing in the macrocosm. Thinking leads us to freedom, and from there to the affirmation of a human love that makes room for objective macrocosmic love in the order of the human. The human is affirmed in its relationship to the cosmos, in its co-creator role.

It is not surprising then that feeling continuously weaves between the two poles. Its beginning activity corresponds to that of both intuition and thinking. And feeling affirms, sustains, and brings to completion both faculties.

Cosmic Thinking

Verse 14, where cosmic thinking is mentioned, appears just after the cusp of the height of summer; it is the first verse of the descending part of the spring/summer cycle. At the other end, cosmic thinking is mentioned in verse 48, at the culmination of the evolution of thinking, emerging out of the winter and after the warning verse (46).

In verse 14 cosmic thinking comes as a gift requiring an attitude of devotion from the human being. In verse 48 it is an acquired capacity. Verse 15 indicates that enchanted weaving wants to bestow strength on us. Verse 16 enjoins us (stern command) to bear inwardly the spirit bounty in order to let the fruits of selfhood emerge. It asks to be mindful of gifts received and how we can integrate them in our destiny journey. Then in 17 cosmic Word can speak in us and a new phase begins.

The pre-Christian principle of ecstasy is transformed through intuition, allowing us to live contained within ourselves and effect those changes that render the gifts of the cosmos able to ripen in us. It's a whole gesture of conscious restraint.

The gifts of cosmic thinking deserve further scrutiny. Referring to this Steiner says: "Man is built up according to the thoughts of the cosmos. The cosmos is the 'great thinker' which down to our last finger-nail engraves our form in us, just as our little thought-work makes its little imprints on our brain every day. . . . As our brain . . . stands under the influence of the work of thinking, so does the whole man stand under the influence of cosmic thinking." And further "in a certain manner we serve [the Hierarchies] so that they may be able to think through us, yet at the same time we are independent beings with identities of our own . . . Cosmic thought is such a regent that we belong with our whole being to that which it has to accomplish."[16] Obviously cosmic thought can direct its activity only in relation to what we offer it by virtue of our karma and our choices. In looking upon the individuals spread out in front of them, we are for the Hierarchies like the individual letters of a book would be for us when we read. "We are links in the thought logic of the cosmos."

At the height of summer we lend ourselves willingly to the Hierarchies thinking through us, and we willingly seek our spirit kinship in them

---

[16] Rudolf Steiner, *Human and Cosmic Thought*, lecture 4.

(verse 13). They, as it were, whisper to us what the future, what world karma needs of us. What they send us by way of suggestion can only emerge in our consciousness in an attitude of devotion indicated in the succeeding verses.

Cosmic thinking can best be understood in relation to the forces of the zodiac in the twelve "schools of thought"/world outlooks.[17] Any given issue can be considered from any of twelve perspectives. These are "fully justifiable standpoints." In between there are transitional perspectives:

Materialism

Mathematism   Sensationalism

Rationalism   Phenomenalism

Idealism   Realism

Psychism   Dynamism

Pneumatism   Monadism

Spiritism

In addition to the twelve outlooks, we can recognize seven planetary soul-moods that color the outlooks:

Gnosis (Saturn)

Logicism (Jupiter)

Voluntarism (Mars)

Empiricism (Sun)

Mysticism (Venus)

Transcendentalism (Mercury)

Occultism (Moon)

Figure 8 summarizes the whole of the outlooks in relation to the soul moods.

---

[17] Rudolf Steiner, *Human and Cosmic Thought*, lecture 3.

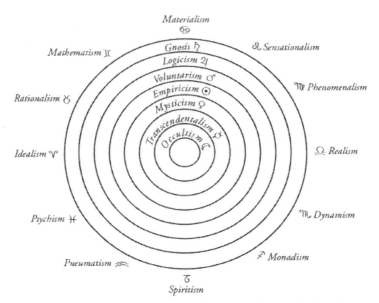

Figure 8: The Outlooks in Relation to the Soul Moods

No outlook or soul mood is bound to an individual for life. Such inclinations/influences can arise before birth or after birth. Steiner offers as an example that of Nietzsche's evolution in time. By virtue of his karma he was so configured that initially the outlook of Idealism could work on him through the soul-mood of Mysticism; he could become a mystical idealist. Later the mood changed to Empiricism in the outlook of Rationalism. Nietzsche changed his relationship to the cosmic thinking of the hierarchies; however, he fell short of his goal and ended up turning his back on his calling.

That cosmic thinking should come toward us "in world appearance" has been something that made me pause and wonder. Some inkling of answer has emerged only from experience with the verses in relation to my biography when a change of direction occurs through the maturation encountered in the summer, and I will put it out tentatively.

When life has been centering on an important decision and theme during the summer months of the year, karmic events present themselves in such a way as to close certain doors and open new ones, if we can seize the moment, though it all may continue to revolve around the same theme. In between the two the soul experiences a certain time of powerlessness. In fact, that a theme disappears and returns in a new form could go completely unperceived. It is only an effort of recollection that brings this matter up to consciousness. It is in this sense that cosmic thinking in sense appearance—through the external events of our biography—may become a reality. It is not a surprise therefore that verse 19 at the end of the Summer Solstice quadrant explicitly asks us to "encompass with memory what I've newly got."

At the other end of the year, cosmic thinking appears in verse 48. This is what we know as fully spiritualized thinking. It is that force which redeems our Self and allows us to fully unite with the powers of nature and the inner world of others. It works from our Spirit Self and no longer divides us from the world and from our fellow human beings. The effort of the soul in developing this spiritualized thinking allows it to meet the sphere of cosmic life when it emerges at the end of winter.

At the summer end of the year the human being lives as if immersed in the cosmic creative thoughts from which the world of appearance takes its expression. Without full awareness the soul is as if immersed in a web of world creative thoughts. At that time the soul is in dialogue with cosmic thoughts that form its spiritual milieu. Intuition offers the soul guidance in the delicate dance of surrender and awareness. Surrender alone would not allow the soul to gather the gifts of cosmic light, cosmic warmth, and cosmic Word. Intuition offers the ego presence necessary. On the other hand too strong an ego presence, without ability to surrender, would preclude the dialogue between soul and world that is the goal of summer's nature consciousness.

At the opposite time of the year self-consciousness gathers what it has received from the creative world thoughts around the kernel of the growing self-awareness. In the sense of Self the receptacle is formed for the Spirit Self and the ascending power of thinking can become cosmic thinking consciously achieved. The power of thinking can consciously unite the human being with the creative forces at work in nature to defy the separation between subject and object and offer a new kind of knowledge that no longer divides.

Cosmic Word

Cosmic Word is one of the central and most encompassing spiritual beings of the Calendar, and one so elusive that it can only be approached tentatively and in stages. Here, and later, we will do so from some of Steiner's lectures, in which cosmic Word is equivalent to the Logos, and from some of his most significant mantras.

"The Word," Steiner indicates, "lies at the very foundation of the whole plan of our creation."[18] What the human being has presently developed—physical, etheric, astral, ego—was once carried by divine spiritual beings, and by what the Bible calls the Logos.

In Old Saturn the Logos was the very first beginning of the physical body. And it is the Logos that is still active in the human being in sleep when the astral and ego desert him. In the Sun period the ether body was added because the Logos became Life upon the Sun. Upon Old Moon the astral body was added, which is a body of light, spiritual light. At this stage life became light; the Logos became Light.

It is in the present cycle of Earth that the human being gained the power to express in sound what lived in his inner life. In the old Moon he had been mute. The power of speech had originally been with the divine, but it was already present in germ within the human being.

During the Earth period the human body was able to confront the Logos as Life and Light because everything became material for him. "And the meaning of life upon Earth is this: That Men should overcome this darkness of the soul, in order that they may recognize the Light of the Logos."[19]

The Logos descended to humanity only once at the time of the Intellectual Soul. The Christ reveals the original and eternal Logos "who works for the unfolding of the Spirit-being of man in the sphere of the Divine Spiritual Being bound up with man from the beginning." And further "Christ's descent is the ensouling of Mankind with the Logos of the beginning

---

[18] *The Gospel of St. John*, lecture 2: *Esoteric Christianity* of May 19, 1908.
[19] The Gospel of St. John, lecture 2: Esoteric Christianity of May 19, 1908.

and of Eternity, whose working for the salvation of Mankind shall never cease."[20]

The ineffable Logos/cosmic Word is present at key moments of the Calendar of the Soul. He is our ultimate destination as much as He is our guide. In the latter function he appears in what is called the First Tablet, which serves as introduction to the lessons of the First Class of the School of Spiritual Science:

O man, know yourself!
Thus speaks the cosmic Word.
You hear it with strength of soul,
You feel it with might of spirit.
Who speaks so powerfully through the world?
Who speaks so tenderly within your heart?
Does it work through the far-spread rays of space
Into your senses' experience of existence?
Does it sound through the weaving waves of time
Into your life's evolving stream?
Is it you, O man, who of yourself,
By sensing in space,
By experiencing in time,
Begets this Word,
Feeling yourself a stranger in the soul-void of space,
Because you lose the force of thinking in the destruction stream of time.

At the height of summer, around St. John, cosmic Word suggests to us the direction to take through cosmic thinking, the combined activity of the hierarchies, which we could call the cosmic intelligence. Here we see cosmic Word "speaking powerfully through the world." At the heights of winter, around Christmas cosmic Word can awaken consciously within us. Here cosmic Word "speaks tenderly within our heart." The Calendar of the Soul is thus a journey through time inviting us to transcend time by meeting the Spirits of the Cycles of Time, which we find in the realm of the First Hierarchy.

---

[20] *Anthroposophical Leading Thoughts*: *A Christmas Study; The Mystery of the Logos.*

Steiner's Life in Relation to Thinking and Intuition/Boding

One of Steiner's major contributions to earth civilization appears in the writings about Goethe's scientific worldview, and is crowned with the publishing of *The Philosophy of Spiritual Activity.*

Steiner's activity of thought is amply documented through his writings. Every step that is required for human beings to transform their thinking is first related to the activity that Goethe accomplished instinctively in his scientific work, in fields such as morphology, plant metamorphosis, and theory of color.

To achieve this goal Steiner captured and described how a phenomenological way of thinking can lead to a science other than the prevailing materialistic science. The point of departure lies in a redemption of thinking. Thinking as is naturally given can lead us to a current science of theories and hypothesis. That is the limit of naturally occurring associative thinking and secondary observations (such as those mediated through microscopes and chemical analysis). The theories are approximations of reality and cannot account for numerous exceptions. Theories build upon other theories and take further departure from reality.

The solution lies not in refining existing theories but in recasting completely our way of thinking in ways that resemble the workings of nature. Thinking must be able to apprehend the living polarities at work in nature and to that end must rise from external sense-bound thinking to imagination, a living kind of thinking that apprehends and transcends all polarities.

All phenomena have equal value, and so-called exceptions or abnormalities are actually windows for a deeper understanding of the polarities at work. From Goethean science we can rise to spiritual science, when we further refine our capacity to consciously research in the spirit that works in all of matter.

The development of this new way of thinking is an objective world necessity. The way in which this emerged in world history is tied to a certain, concrete world karma to which Steiner had to attune himself. Had all things developed in the best of scenarios, Karl Julius Schröer, the reincarnated Plato, would have been able to take on the work of Goethe and transform it into the spiritual scientific method. Indeed all the doors were already open for Schröer to accomplish this world-deed.

When the time came for the scientific Goethe to be brought back to the world in a transformed fashion, an obstacle arose in Schröer's resistance, and ultimately unwillingness, to accomplish his task. He would not discipline his thinking through the crucible of the intellect; he remained content to intuit Goethe's greatness without offering to the world a way to accomplish in full consciousness what the 18th-century genius had done instinctively. Steiner, who had already awakened to his own mission, decided to take on Schröer's world task and postpone his own. This is something worth a closer look in relation to what was brought forth earlier in the chapter. It illustrates how intuition worked in Steiner's life.

Steiner had recognized the greatness of Schröer's individuality; he had known that with him lay an exalted task and possibility. He had been inwardly annoyed by the great man's complacency and resistance and expressed these in at times humorous fashion in his biography. At the same time Steiner was keenly listening to what the future of humanity required of him. We could say that Steiner was himself a conscious thought in the cosmic thinking of the hierarchies; that a new possibility was offered to him in freedom and he embraced it.

Steiner was uniquely placed to hear what the spiritual world saw as an objective need for humanity. He was listening both to world karma and to his inner soul life. He was able to let go of his own priorities, and to let come of what objective world karma required of him. This change can be understood in relation to Steiner saying he would have originally worked at conveying spiritual experiences as they presented themselves to him. Now he had to illustrate each step of his process of thinking.[21]

In Steiner cosmic thinking fully achieved met with the cosmic thinking of the hierarchies as in a conversation between pure spiritual beings. Due to his desire to contribute to world karma, he now accepted to work from wholly different outlooks and soul moods; to not just impart spiritual reality as it manifested itself to him, but meet the prevailing materialistic/sensation-based outlook of the times and forge a phenomenological path

---

[21] For a further development of this theme see Luigi Morelli, *Karl Julius Schröer and Rudolf Steiner: Anthroposophy and the Teachings of Karma and Reincarnation*, Chapter 1: Karl Julius Schröer's and Rudolf Steiner's Missions.

that could be followed by others. To that end he had to carefully observe his thinking processes as they emerged, understand their unfolding and detail the steps that all individual beings can take in replicating the experience. The book *The Philosophy of Spiritual Activity* is exactly that, the path of a given individual, but also the path possible to all other individuals at the time of the consciousness soul.

CHAPTER 3

COSMIC LIFE, COSMIC LIGHT, AND COSMIC WARMTH

The Calendar of the Soul leads us through the ethers, which are gateways for the realm of the cosmic Word. The calendar speaks most of life and cosmic life (life of worlds, strength of life, life of man, man's being, spirit life, germinating force of soul, maternal life, etc.) around the times of the equinoxes, of cosmic light and warmth around the Summer Solstice. The explicit mention of "cosmic Word" weaves in the verses around both solstices. These terms reappear metamorphosed in the fall-winter time of the year.

Moving through the Ethers

As we have seen, on earth we have warmth, airy and watery states, and the earth element; on the other side of the threshold life ether (the highest), sound ether, light ether, and warmth ether. In *Christ and the Human Soul* Steiner reveals that what the human being takes within himself from the external world he deadens; this is the case with the warmth, the air he exhales, or the light that enters through his senses.[22] We cannot kill, however, the sound ether and the life ether, but this means that we cannot partake of their essence as much as we do with the light and warmth ethers. In the Calendar of the Soul the two ethers together, and what rays

---

[22] Rudolf Steiner, *Christ and the Human Soul*, lecture of July 16, 1914.

from them out of the realm of the First Hierarchy, is called "cosmic life." Likewise we find cosmic light and warmth to encompass and transcend light ether and warmth ether.

Death was the gift of the Gods when the human being had to undergo the Luciferic temptation. It penetrated our physical body in the lower ethers, those of light and warmth, not the two higher ones. This is what is meant in the biblical "Of the tree of life [the human being] shall not eat." In occult terms this could be extended to mean "Of the tree of life [the human being] shall not eat and the Spirit of Matter [Harmony of the Spheres] he shall not hear!"[23]

Warmth and light are accessible to the human being through sense-perception; not so the sound and life ethers. The workings of the sound ether only manifest themselves within the life processes. The life ether cannot be perceived, only its effects on living beings. For present science, life itself remains a riddle.

During sleep the astral body is permeated by the forces of the Harmony of the Spheres; these bring order to what has been produced in waking life through the sense impressions. But the human being has lost the experience of the sublime cosmic life and harmony of the spheres.

Christ came precisely from those cosmic regions from which the human being had been closed off, regions that still belonged to the human being in the primeval state of innocence preceding the Fall. The two regions (higher ethers) were withdrawn so that the human being may not suffer their death too. To these his soul truly belongs. This is the world closest to original participation that the human being enters through the yearly reenactment of Easter. It is stated most eloquently in verse 3: "Thus to the World-All speaks, in self-forgetfulness and mindful of its primal state the growing human I." World-All is thus the expression of a world larger than what we perceive, which is our birthright, but which we have foregone through the Fall. This sets the tone for the spring-summer half of the year.

---

[23] Rudolf Steiner, *Christ and the Human Soul*, lecture of July 16, 1914

Transformation of the Ethers

Steiner indicates that clairvoyantly seen:

> The light dips down into the plants and rises again out of them as a living spiritual element. In the animals it is the chemical ether that enters, and this chemical ether is not perceptible to man; if he could be aware of it, it would sound forth spiritually. The animals transform this ether into water-spirits. The plants transform light into air-spirits; animals transform the spirit active in the chemical ether into water-spirits.

And further:

> Clairvoyant sight perceives how man sends out his moral, intellectual and aesthetic aura into the world, and how this aura continues to live as earthly spirit in the spirituality of the Earth. As a comet draws its tail through the Cosmos, so does man draw through the whole of earthly life the spiritual aura which he projects. This spiritual aura is held together, phantom-like, during a man's life, but at the same time it rays out into the world his moral and intellectual properties of soul.[24]

Since shortly before the time of Golgotha into this spiritual aura the human being also brought in the death element, that which he develops in killing the light and the warmth. Without Golgotha he would have carried into this aura his "objective guilt and objective sin" without being able to add to these the essences of the Music of the Spheres and the Cosmic Life. When we operate out of "Not I but Christ in me," what we ray out of us has the capacity to become enlivened again

The human being, permeated by the Christ impulse, can return to his full potential, to being the soul which the divine beings originally meant him to be. Christ restores the human being to his true cosmic home, which

---

[24] Rudolf Steiner, *Christ and the Human Soul*, lecture of July 16, 1914.

he relinquished through the Luciferic temptation. He guides us back to our original home in the spirit. All these notions of primeval home are echoed in the first calendar verses of spring. It is fitting that these ideas and yearnings are expressed and felt in the soul just right after the yearly reenactment of the Mystery of Golgotha at Easter.

When the soul unites itself at Easter with the Christ, it feels a vivifying element; it experiences a transition from death to life. The resurrection of nature is automatic; that of the human being only if he has united himself with the Christ impulse. It is through the Christ, and through our choice to make room for Him in our soul, that "we can receive, by proxy as it were, that which would otherwise come to us from the Music of the Spheres and the Cosmic Life."[25]

Cosmic Life, Cosmic Light and Cosmic Warmth

We will look at the calendar through the lens of the thirteen crosses, starting from the first two quadrants. We find crosses 1 to 3 closest to the equinoxes and the festivals of Easter and Michaelmas. Here is the pole of cosmic life that takes the ascendancy. It is expressed around the Spring Equinox and Easter in a multitude of expressions: sprouting growth, cosmic life, joy of growth, strength of life, germinating power, and so on.

When we move toward the Summer Solstice, we penetrate gradually the light ether. A remarkable reminder of this is found in the verses of cross 5 (5, 22, 31, 48), which have been called the light verses. Each of the verses' first lines makes direct reference to light from the heights or from the depths. Other expressions around this time of the year include floods of light, world's enticing light, and lose myself in light.

While the theme of cosmic light continues, cosmic warmth is mentioned in verses 9 and 12 with expressions such as cosmic warmth and spirit's fiery worlds in verse 13. Cosmic Word is referred to either explicitly and directly or indirectly from crosses 10 to 13 (verses 10 to 17).

The same could be said of the fall and winter quadrants of the year, but here the ethers are expressed no longer in the life of nature and the cosmos

---

[25] Rudolf Steiner, *Christ and the Human Soul,* lecture of July 16, 1914

but in the way in which the human being sends out his moral, intellectual, and aesthetic aura into the world. We will return to this theme.

A special place is taken in the calendar by cross 7. The sphere of cosmic life is found in the crosses preceding cross 7; that of cosmic warmth in the verses following (8 to 13), cosmic light appears on both sides of the threshold. As previously mentioned cross 7 divides the year in four equal parts. And it forms a threshold within each quadrant, where it occurs at the exact middle point. Verse 7 stands at the midpoint of 1 and 13 (spring quadrant); the same is true of 20 in relation to 14 and 26 (summer quadrant), 33 in relation to 27 and 39 (fall quadrant), and 46 in relation to 40 to 52 (winter quadrant).

The Verses of Cross 7: Looking Backward and Forward

The threshold verses are axes around which the Calendar of the Soul revolves, just like the equinoxes and the solstices. We will use them in differentiating four kinds of soul faculties throughout the year. Each verse indicates both a danger and what is needed to avert it and/or look at the past and the future.

Verse 46 warns us of the danger of the effect of the call of the senses on the forces of the soul and calls us to remember the effort accomplished during the winter. It calls on the power of memory:

> The world is threatening to stun
> The inborn forces of my soul;
> Now, memory, come forth
> From spirit depths, enkindling light;
> Invigorate my inward sight
> Which only by the strength of will
> Is able to sustain itself.

Verse 7 indicates that now it is the self that tends to lose itself in the light, a little like in the ecstasy of midsummer that preceded the Christ event. Here it is boding/intuition that is called forth as the faculty that places us in a dialogue between self and world in which the self does not lose its grounding:

My Self is threatening to fly forth,
Lured strongly by the world's enticing light.
Come forth now, prophetic feeling [boding],
Take up with strength your rightful task:
Replace in me the power of thought
Which in the senses' glory
Would gladly lose itself.

Verse 20 looks back and establishes the success in remaining connected to the self: "I feel at last my life's reality." And it points us to our coming task: now that we feel the budding selfhood power within, we can establish a relationship with the wider world of which the self is a citizen in order not to wither within ourselves:

I feel at last my life's reality
Which, severed from the world's existence,
Would in itself obliterate itself,
And building only on its own foundation,
Would in itself bring death upon itself.

Verse 33 indicates first of all that we have been successful because we "feel at last the world's reality," and it challenges us to deepen this communion and the ability to re-create this reality in our souls in order to become co-creators:

I feel at last the world's reality
Which, lacking the communion of my soul,
Would by itself be frosty, empty life,
And showing itself powerless
To recreate itself in souls,
Would in itself find only death.

The Calendar of the Soul Year in Relation to the Natural Year

The threshold verses occur in the exact middle of a quadrant, but these are offset from the mid-season verses by about three verses. Yet, there is an organic relationship between each set of verses. Each warning verse sets out a question, which receives a first answer in the exact mid-season verse of the next season, 10 weeks later in the weeks that cover May 1 (Beltane), August 1 (Lammas Day), October 31–November 1 (Samhain, All Souls). and February 2 (Candlemas, Imbolc). Let us see how.

Verses 7 and 17: Intuition/boding works from verses 7 to 17 and allows the person not "to lose himself" in the senses' glory. It is cosmic Word that rescues us after 10 weeks in verse 17 (July 28–August 3). Intuition leads the way to the cosmic Word, which continues the work of divining of intuition by now speaking to the soul. The inner voice of intuition is strengthened by the voice of the Word:

> Thus speaks the cosmic Word
> That I by grace through senses' portals
> Have led into my innermost soul:
> Imbue your spirit depths
> With my wide world horizons
> To find in future time myself in you.

Verses 20 and 30: My desire to unite with the world's existence and find life more abundant (20) is met in bringing the sun of the world in my soul and in harmonizing thinking and feeling in verse 30. The same union of opposites is expressed in the summer of the soul reached in winter:

> There flourish within the sunlight of my soul
> The ripened fruits of thinking;
> To conscious self-assurance
> The flow of feeling is transformed.
> I can perceive now joyfully
> The autumn's spirit-waking:

The winter will arouse in me
The summer of the soul.

Verses 33 and 43

The theme of cold and separation of 33 is met with glowing warmth, forces of the heart, and inner fire in 43. The summer of the soul is reached in winter.

The soul is impelled to let the world into itself so that it can co-create and renew world existence (33). In 43 the soul has attained part of this goal. It has the strength of heart to give being to the world of appearance. It can bid defiance to the apparently cold world because it has achieved conscious participation in its life:

In winter's depths is kindled
True spirit life with glowing warmth;
It gives to world appearance,
Through forces of the heart, the power to be.
Grown strong, the human soul defies
With inner fire the coldness of the world.

Verses 46 and 4: The forces of the soul threaten to go their own way. They are held together by memory and strength of will (46). The invigorating of inward sight becomes the ability to sense kinship with the sun-illumined world in verse 4. The union of the forces of the soul is achieved in thinking uniting with feeling through the activated will. And this also brings about the union of man and world:

I sense a kindred nature to my own:
Thus speaks perceptive feeling
As in the sun-illuminated world
It merges with the floods of light;
To thinking's clarity
My feeling would give warmth
And firmly bind as one
The human being and the world.

The Turning Points of the Threshold Verses

In light of the above we will look at that interval that covers the threshold verse and up to any of the corresponding verses just mentioned: the intervals 4 to 7, 17 to 20, 30 to 33, and 43 to 46.

Spring to Summer: Verses 4 to 7
Verse 7 is a true warning verse. The danger is the Luciferic possibility of losing ourselves in the light [and warmth]:

> My self is threatening to fly forth [the self which has been strengthened
> through the course of fall and winter],
> Lured strongly by the world's enticing light.
> Come forth, prophetic feeling,
> Take up with strength your rightful task:
> Replace in me the power of thought
> Which in the senses' glory
> Would gladly lose itself.

In verse 4 is expressed the desire to integrate thinking and feeling and unite the human being with the world. The light verse, 5, expands our consciousness toward the cosmos and moves us beyond our narrow confines of self. This becomes a surprisingly, seemingly sudden, widened consciousness of the connection between microcosm and macrocosm in 6. However, in between we have been blessed by the flooding of light manifesting externally in 4, and through the gods' creative work in 5.

The danger of verse 6 arises from the particular nature of the Gemini experience in the zodiac. It's as if a portal opened and the human being were permitted to divine the world behind it, the world of the cosmic Word. Then the portal closes, leaving the human being enriched. This window over the world of the spirit possibly explains the overwhelming, experience of verse 6. For this reason we are then reminded of the danger of "the world's enticing light" and the danger of the self flying forth. The threshold verse offers us the solution to the challenge in the development of the new force of "intuition" to replace the power of thought (7). And the goal of this warning is revealed in 8 with the possibility of uniting with the godly being who is coming toward us.

Summer to Fall: 17 to 20

In verse 17 the cosmic Word has spoken within the soul. The response of the human being is one of expansion and desire for purification (18). What has been received by the human being in summer in a state of dream has to be called forth consciously through memory (19).

Verse 20 calls us to explore the needs of the world:

I feel at last my life's reality [the Self I was risking losing in 7]
Which, severed from the world's existence,
Would in itself obliterate itself,
And building only on its own foundation,
Would in itself bring death upon itself.

Immediately after selfhood, forces can be cultivated and start to be felt in conscious expectation (21). In between (verse 20) the human being who has been dreaming can awaken to his life's reality and seek consciously to unite to the world's existence, no longer uniting with it as in an original participation. Memory of what has just happened forms a bridge to a more conscious participation.

The desire to stir memory to review what we have experienced becomes the sowing of a seed surrounded by light of expectation in 21. This becomes promise of the summer of the soul in verse 23.

Fall to Winter: 30 to 33

More than a warning verse, 33 is a verse alerting us to the larger needs of the world; it asks us to go beyond ourselves to meet the objective needs of the macrocosm:

I feel at last the world's reality [goal of verse 20]
Which, lacking the communion of my soul,
Would by itself, be frosty, empty life,
And showing itself powerless
To recreate itself in souls,
Would in itself find only death.

In verse 30 we have obtained the seeds for an integration of feeling and thinking, which was first sought in 4. Thinking and feeling support each other and prepare us confidently for the winter and its awakening task.

The integration of thinking and feeling of 30 gives us strength and insight into the weaving of life's destiny and, no doubt, confidence in 32. This confidence in self alerts us and warns us to the larger needs of the world in the threshold verse 33. We can now feel the world's reality, decide to unite with and contribute to it. This has a direct effect in 34. What was strength and insight in 32 in uniting us with the world (33) becomes now inwardly a new sense of self and outwardly cosmic forces pouring into our deeds; in 34 we realize that we can experience true existence. Verse 34 restates 32 with greater emphasis by adding "new risen sense of Self" (before this it was simply "my own force" in 32) and our ability to pour "cosmic forces" into our deeds.

Winter to Spring: 43 to 46

This is once more a true warning verse. The arrival of the realm of cosmic life can overwhelm the soul, dissolve it:

The world is threatening to stun
The inborn forces of my soul;
Now, memory, come forth
From spirit depths, enkindling light;
Invigorate my inward sight
Which only by the strength of will
Is able to sustain itself.

The confident power of thinking that has established itself through the fall and winter is now conscious of its co-creator role in the Earth's evolution. It knows it can "give the world of appearance the power to be" (43). Thinking has recognized its kinship with the formative forces in nature, hence the assertion that it can "fill the world's bewildering, sprouting growth with the [its] creative will" (44). In verse 45 the soul can, through the power of thought, desire "union with the world's becoming."

The approach of the spring leads to the eventual, gradual waning of thinking and with it the danger of the separation of the soul forces under the appeal of the senses. Once more, as in verse 19 it is memory that is called forth to counter the danger. Whereas in verse 19, memory has a nurturing, enveloping quality, here we find it united with strength of will in the act of enkindling light. The memory of all that thinking has developed through the journey through sleep, and darkness serves to meet the joy of growth with the will in thinking; to create the capacity in cosmic thinking for the meeting and recognition of the two forces that share a same origin; the formative forces in nature and thinking in the human being (48). This leads to the achievement of cosmic thinking, which will become revelation in 51. Clarity of thought recognizes the force of cosmic life in 49, just as boding recognizes the floods of light in 4 (the two are verses of cross 4).

Verse 45 reminds us of the spirit-birth (first heard in verse 38 of Christmas) and the importance of thinking for conscious participation for those who want to feel united with the world. When the world threatens to stun the forces of the soul through the impact on the senses (46), we must cultivate memory and kindle inner light. This means strengthening the force of thought through cosmic powers. Where this leads is indicated with "certainty of cosmic thinking" and the "awakening of love" in 48.

The threshold verses form turning points in the course of the year to such an extent that it is justified to divide the course of the year according to these axes thus:

- 7 to 19: spring to summer quadrant (Summer Solstice quadrant)
- 20 to 32: summer to fall quadrant (Fall Equinox quadrant)
- 33 to 45: fall to winter quadrant (Winter Solstice quadrant)
- 46 to 6: winter to spring quadrant (Spring Equinox quadrant)

To this we will turn in the next chapters. We will first look at themes that group around the Summer Solstice, those that gather around the Winter Solstice, and those that gather around the Spring and Fall equinoxes.

In the following chapters we will refer to the solstice and equinox quadrants. In order to embrace more closely their particular nature, we will look at another differentiating criterion: the experience of self during the year as it presents itself in each quadrant. For the sake of clarity we will start from the end of winter and with the achievement that is the sense of Self.

Experience of the Self through the Year

Karl König refers to the time before incarnating in which the human soul lives in the revelation of spiritual beings, but with little awareness of their distinct identities. At this point gradually arises a strong sense of self. Whereas knowledge of the spiritual world recedes in its richness, the soul perceives more fully its own separateness and individuality. This is what in fact triggers the longing for existence and the soul's new incarnation.

The sense of self can come to fruition through the ascent of the power of thinking. This leads to the conscious recognition of the cosmic Word. König concludes, "Thus the sense of self is like a cup or chalice created by the force of thinking, and so it becomes the bearer of the highest forces of the spirit."[26] It becomes the bearer of the cosmic Word in the sense of "not I but Christ in me."

The sense of self has its birth in the consciousness soul but arrives to completion in the Spirit Self, as Rudolf Steiner indicates in *Theosophy*: "The consciousness soul merely touches the autonomous truth that is independent of all sympathy and antipathy, but the spirit self carries this same truth inside itself, taken up, enclosed and individualized by means of the 'I' and taken into the individual's independent being. Through becoming independent and uniting with the truth, the 'I' itself achieves immortality."[27]

We will now retrace the journey from the ego to the sense of Self. To do that we will look at each quadrant, and divide each quadrant in the time before and after each solstice and equinox. We will start the cycle in spring after the sense of Self, achieved in the winter, is retreating.

---

[26] Karl König, *The Calendar of the Year: A Commentary*, 242.
[27] Rudolf Steiner, *Theosophy*, Chapter 1 (The Essential Nature of the Human Being), heading iv: (Body, Soul and Spirit).

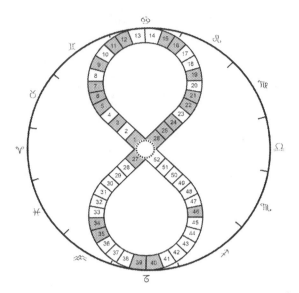

Figure 9: Experience of the Ego/Self/Sense of Self through the Year

Spring Equinox Quadrant: 46 to 7

Verses 46 to 52 (before the Spring Equinox)

In verse 46 (threshold verse) we have the possibility of the Ahrimanic temptation; the world threatening to stun the soul. In verse 50 the joy of growth speaks to the human ego:

> Thus to the human ego speaks
> In mighty revelation,
> Unfolding its inherent forces,
> The joy of growth throughout the world:
> I carry into you my life
> From its enchanted bondage
> And so attain my true goal.

This is an interesting and sudden transition from the experience of Self and sense of Self of the Winter Solstice quadrant, and it comes after ten verses without direct reference to them. The Self will first appear in the verse that is complementary to 50: verse 3, though an indirect reminder first appears in the Easter verse.

. . . Then rising from the sheath of self,
Thoughts soar to distances of space
And dimly bind man's being to the spirit's life.

The self is here mentioned only in relation to its sheath, where achieved thinking has its seat. Otherwise it plays no active role.

Verses 1 to 7 (after the Spring Equinox)
During this time of the year the same self that was the achievement in the first half of winter is considered something to be overcome in light of the original realm of cosmic life from which Christ precedes and from which humanity has its being. In verse 3:

Thus to the World-All speaks,
In self-forgetfulness
And mindful of its primal state,
The growing human I:
In you, if I can free myself
From fetters of my selfhood,
I fathom my essential being.

All of a sudden the work the soul has invested in polishing the self appears insufficient. But this is only because the coming of the Christ makes us measure ourselves against the archetype of humanity before the Fall.

Verse 5 familiarizes us with a variation of many in the term of narrow selfhood's inner power:

Within the light that out of spirit depths
Weaves germinating power into space
And manifests the gods' creative work:
Within its shine, the soul's true being
Is widened into worldwide life
And resurrected
From narrow selfhood's inner power.

The soul that is resurrected, amplified into a larger realm of existence, longs for the perfection that can only be reached beyond earth. In the next verse the soul sees its limitations and measures both its own shortcomings and the apparently unlimited potential of the Self. This occurs at the time of Ascension in which the soul can most closely feel the realm of the etheric in which lives the new Christ revelation:

> There has arisen from its narrow limits
> My self and finds itself
> As revelation of all worlds
> Within the sway of time and space;
> The world, as archetype divine,
> Displays to me at every turn
> The truth of my own likeness.

Here the human I experiences the reality of its higher self; the I experiences itself as being made in the image of God. It feels its kinship with the cosmic Self and intuits the possibility to journey toward it. This is an answer to verse 3 where the I has evoked a memory of its primeval being in the World-All. Now its sees not just its origin but its destination. In this natural expansion lies the danger of the Luciferic temptation that will be rendered explicit in verse 7, one of the threshold verses. The soul can intuit the boundless dimension of the Self but cannot as yet live at that level. Here is offered the antidote to the temptation, when thinking cannot guide us through the spring and summer time of that year. The power of intuition has to laboriously emerge and find its way. Verse 7 reminds us that in order to be held within itself, the soul needs new strength.

Summer Solstice Quadrant: 7 to 20

> *7 to 13 (before the Summer Solstice)*
> Verse 9 inaugurates the new theme of losing oneself:

> When I forget the narrow will of self,
> The cosmic warmth that heralds summer's glory
> Fills all my soul and spirit;
> To lose myself in light
> Is the behest of spirit vision

And intuition tells me strongly:
O lose yourself to find yourself.

Forgetting narrow will of self, qualified by "when," indicates the end of a process (as we see in verses 3, 5, and 6). It calls us a step further to sacrifice ourselves by losing ourselves in light. Verses 9 to 12 indicate the theme of sacrifice of the Self. Verse 11 continues the theme of losing oneself:

In this the sun's high hour it rests
With you to understand these words of wisdom:
Surrendered to the beauty of the world,
Be stirred with new-enlivened feeling;
The human I can lose itself
And find itself within the cosmic I.
The verse goes a step further from losing, specifying what the human soul can find. So does verse 12:

The radiant beauty of the world
Compels my inmost soul to free
God-given powers of my nature
That they may soar into the cosmos,
To take wing from myself
And trustingly to seek myself
In cosmic light and cosmic warmth.

When cosmic warmth adds itself to cosmic light, the soul approaches the realms of the cosmic Word. In fact it is the cosmic Word, who speaks to the soul that is yet unaware of its presence in verse 13.

14 to 20 (after the Summer Solstice)
Verse 14 recaps the soul's journey from 7 to 13: "dreamlike thinking seemed to daze and rob me of myself." And it announces the goal of the sacrifice: the arrival of cosmic thinking, the thinking of the hierarchies in us. The hierarchies want, as it were, to enlarge our being, though this can only be taken up by the human being in freedom in verse 15:

I feel enchanted weaving
Of spirit within outer glory.
In dullness of the senses
It has enwrapt my being
In order to bestow the strength
Which in its narrow bounds my I
Is powerless to give itself.

The I stands as if powerless, needing to be fructified from above and without. To the sacrifice must correspond the willingness to empty and cleanse oneself of all vain desires of the soul in order to connect with that Self that was prematurely felt in verse 6, just before the threshold verse:

To bear in inward keeping spirit bounty
Is stern command of my prophetic feeling [intuition],
That ripened gifts divine
Maturing in the depths of soul
To selfhood bring their fruits.

From now on intuition calls us to a new task: to nurture and tend to the growth of what lies still concealed within the soul, because it is undergoing a slow but steady growth. The soul must be guarded from hurrying the process as we are reminded in verse 19:

In secret to encompass now
With memory what I've newly got
Shall be my striving's further aim:
Thus, ever strengthening, selfhood's forces
Shall be awakened from within
And growing, give me to myself.

In this second part of the quadrant, just after the Summer Solstice, the soul nurtures the selfhood forces growing within. All is done in light of the future. What has been received before and by midsummer lies dormant in the soul. Our outward passivity is in reality a kind of receptive activity of the soul, a patient sensing and nurturing of what wants to grow. It is a kind of pregnancy of the soul that has to be accompanied with reverence and care.

Fall Equinox Quadrant: 20 to 33

20 to 26 (before the Fall Equinox)
Verse 20 forms a call to cultivate our higher self and not to build on our lower self alone, now that we have received the light of cosmic Word and integrated it in our soul. Just after the threshold verse, intuition that is about to fulfill its task follows with interest what is to become of the emerging selfhood power (verse 21):

I feel strange power, bearing fruit
And gaining strength to give myself to me.
I sense the seed maturing
And expectation [intuition], light-filled, weaving
Within me on my selfhood's power.

That selfhood should appear as strange can make us wonder. That this is so we are reminded by Steiner in the soul's experience in the life after death the first approach of our higher self is experienced as something so large as to feel foreign (used in other translations instead of "strange") to ourselves. The selfhood power appears for the last time after "fruits of selfhood" and "selfhood's forces" of the second half of the Summer Solstice quadrant. In verse 22 a step is taken from selfhood forces and power to the expression of Self. However, it is still placed in the future:

The light from world-wide spaces
Works on within with living power;
Transformed to light of soul
It shines into the spirit depths
To bring to birth the fruits
Whereby out of the self of worlds
The human self in course of time shall ripen.

Verse 24 marks an important transition: awareness of Self arises in the soul, a conscious step of what was only a prefiguration in verse 6, awakening the desire for self-cognition:

Unceasingly itself creating
Soul life becomes aware of self;
The cosmic spirit, striving on,
Renews itself by self-cognition,
And from the darkness of the soul
Creates the fruit of self-engendered will.

Just before Michaelmas the soul feels something more than a power growing within. It awakens to the full realization of the self. Verse 26 of Michaelmas forms another turning point:

O Nature, your maternal life
I bear within the essence of my will.
And my will's fiery energy
Shall steel my spirit striving,
That sense of self springs forth from it
To hold me in myself.

The sense of Self is felt like a promise (a birth) that will hold me in myself in the future. The bridge is cast between consciousness soul and spirit self that will lead to the spirit-birth at Christmas.

27 to 32 (after the Fall Equinox)
As in verse 21, but now a step further (from selfhood power to Self) intuition that was light-filled expectation in 21 detects the Self as gift of summer sun in verse 27:

When to my being's depths I penetrate,
There stirs expectant longing [intuition]
That self-observing, I may find myself
As gift of summer sun, a seed
That warming lives in autumn mood
As germinating force of soul.

Thinking and the growing realization of the Self illumine the soul with light through the winter.

Winter Solstice Quadrant: 33 to 46

33 to 39 (before the Winter Solstice)

In verse 38, the cosmic Word, made conscious in the soul, presides over the spirit-birth in the human soul. Cosmic Word appears in fact from verse 36; when it emerges at Christmas the ground has been prepared for the momentous birth. The Spirit Self touches the soul. In verse 39 the sense of Self is an attainment of what was only announced in 26 and 27:

Surrendering to spirit revelation
I gain the light of cosmic being;
The power of thinking, growing clearer,
Gains strength to give myself to me,
And quickening there frees itself
From thinker's energy my sense of Self.

The fire of Whitsun is now an inner fire in verse 40. Here we see that the cosmic Word has a cleansing and refining power over the Self:

And when I live in spirit depths
And dwell within my soul's foundations,
There streams from love-worlds of the heart,
To fill the vain delusion of the self,
The fiery power of the cosmic Word.

Verses 26 and 39 bring a powerful experience in the light of cosmic being [universal life]. Verse 26 announces the yearning of the soul to incarnate more fully; verse 39 marks the time of incarnation out of the spirit, just after Christmas. This is the sense of the expression sense of Self. Verse 40 echoes in "love-worlds of the heart" the Michaelmas verse's expression "my will's fiery energy." Thinking is now pervaded by the force of will. And that entails the necessity to "fill the vain delusion of my Self."

40 to 46 (after the Winter Solstice)

Only two verses before the solstice mention the Self in the Winter Solstice quadrant, but others mention the cosmic Word and the growing clarity of thinking. Surprisingly, nothing is mentioned after the solstice itself though we see a growth from the freedom given by thinking's role and the soul's capacity to develop and act as a co-creator in the plan of creation. The Self prepares itself for a new beginning. It can no longer grow. It has to change in its inner orientation to the world in reaching for the time of Easter and spring through the annual recurrence of the Mystery of Golgotha.

Let's briefly review the journey of the self through the year. Around the Spring Equinox we go from the human ego to the Self as an intimation standing far ahead of itself. Mostly the theme is that of overcoming fetters and narrow limits of selfhood through the power of intuition in the second part of the quadrant, just after Easter. Thinking confirms what it has already achieved. It is through thinking that we can seek union with the world's becoming; it is through thinking that we can withstand the onslaught of the world upon the forces of the soul. After that, through thinking we can serenely meet the joy of growth. With certainty of cosmic thinking we can awaken love and hope. In a crowning gesture the joy of growth can become revelation in the ego and itself attain its desired evolutionary goal.

The time of the Summer Solstice is divided in two parts: before the solstice (really verse 13), losing self to find self; after the solstice, seeing the power of selfhood emerge and nurturing it within through the power of intuition.

The Fall Equinox culminates in an awareness of Self in the soul and in the nurturing of the budding sense of Self. Intuition accompanies the movement by confirming what comes from the past and taking leave of the human being. The power of thinking ascends. Thinking's power grows as the inner light and summer of the soul.

Around the Winter Solstice we see the maturation of the sense of Self accompanying the spirit-birth of cosmic Word in the human soul at Christmas. After verse 40 the Self is present only through its deeds and through cosmic Word that fills it. Warmth of heart and love are mentioned in its stead. At this time the spirit worlds seek themselves in the human being filled with the power of the cosmic Word.

In the next chapters we will further the exploration of the calendar around a multitude of themes that relate most closely to equinox or solstice times. The amplitude and variety of themes and their interweaving can obscure the element of continuity that exists from month to month and verse to verse in the calendar. For this reason Appendix 1 gives those who begin to explore the calendar an overview of the themes that unite groups of verses and the subtle links between one verse and the following.

CHAPTER 4

SUMMER SOLSTICE THEMES

In this chapter and the next ones we intend to look at each of the mid-season quadrants and the themes that weave around each solstice and equinox times. This approaches continues the thematic approach that I have first met in the work of Karl König. The Calendar of the Soul presents a large number of interweaving themes that surge, fade, and metamorphose. So many in fact that it is easy to lose oneself in the agile, intricate, and surprising harmonies that play in the symphony of the year. I believe this ordering has been made possible through König's key recognition of the two halves of the year and the forces at play therein. It is because we have previously looked at the place of intuition, thinking, and ego/self that a new order starts to emerge from the myriad of strands that form the tapestry of the calendar.

The themes that will emerge are but some of many. When looking at one strand we will mention in passing how it interweaves with others, at the risk of some repetition. I hope this will encourage the reader and meditant to recognize and explore many possible new threads.

Since we are placing this exploration under the theme of the cardinal events of the sun's path and the accompanying Christian festivals, we will also refer to these and in fact place them at the center of our considerations. Rudolf Steiner offered us potent imaginations for each of the turning points of the seasons: Easter, St. John, Michaelmas, and Christmas. We will first look at the St. John imagination and contrast it with the Christmas imagination in the next chapter, then turn to the solstices with Easter and Michaelmas.

The St. John Imagination

As summer approaches, Steiner indicates that the elemental beings are drawn more and more out of the earth, and their activities and movements are influenced by planetary movements. So is the human being led out of himself to enter into the "doings of the planets."[28]

In summer the organism is permeated by the suphur process, which can be equated to a combustion process. Due to this, seen from the cosmos, the inner being of the individual begins to shine. But this also attracts the Ahrimanic beings, wanting to draw her into a state of half-conscious sleep and dream.

Just as in winter the limestone, deeply in the earth, is "inwardly contented," so is Nature in summer when it is at its most active. The human being acquires a kind of nature consciousness. He feels himself spread out over the whole of nature. The cosmos wants to bring the spiritual to meet the human being out of nature's life and expansiveness. Whereas in winter we have matter permeated with spirit, in summer the spirit is woven through with matter. We could say that the spirit draws matter to itself; it clothes itself with matter.

Down within the Earth the crystalline forms, colored in deep blue, take the forms of lines, angles, and surfaces and reach their greatest beauty. These influences are sent toward human consciousness. The blue is interwoven with lines that sparkle like silver. And the human being feels a part of it: "One feels that as a human form one has grown out of the blue depths of the earth's crust." What lives in this crystalline matrix is cosmic will.

In the heights one perceives what corresponds to cosmic intelligence alive everywhere and woven within the light; it is the intelligence of many beings who live together and within each other. The elemental beings, rising upward from the Earth, blend themselves with this shining intelligence. This is the polar opposite of cosmic will.

A form appears up above, the countenance that emerges shining warmly out of the surrounding radiant cosmic intelligence. It is the form of Uriel, "whose own intelligence arises fundamentally from the working

---

[28] What follows is taken from Rudolf Steiner, *Four Seasons and the Archangels*, lecture 4 of October 12, 1923.

together of the planetary forces of our planetary system, supported by the working of the fixed stars of the Zodiac."

The stern gaze of Uriel is directed downwards to the blue silver crystalline lattice, because here he discerns the disturbing shapes that continuously form and dissolve. These shapes are due to human errors that disturb the natural order, and in Uriel's gaze we can recognize the weaving together of what is natural and what is moral. Human virtues, on the other hand, rise up with the silver gleaming lines toward the cloud-like formations that envelop Uriel, who raises arm-like wings in admonition.

Uriel gathers these impulses to offer to the human being the possibility of historic consciousness. The silver-blue lattice is gathered with human errors around the figure of the Earth Mother (in blue), Demeter or Mary. What flows above, on the other hand, can be experienced as the Spirit Father. And between the two arises the form of the Son, completing the Imagination of the Trinity:

> [The human being] feels himself no longer sundered from the world around him, but placed within it, united above with the shining Intelligence, in which he experiences, as in the womb of worlds, his own best thoughts. He feels himself united below, right into his bony system, with the cosmic crystallizing force—and again the two united with one another. He feels his death united with the spirit-life of the universe; and he feels how this spirit-life craves to awaken the crystal forces and the silver-gleaming life in the midst of earthly death.

This could be summarized as the human being in the Mysteries of the Middle between the Mysteries of the Heights and the Mysteries of the Depths.

The early spring is the time of overcoming of narrow boundaries of self—a theme to which we will return in the equinoxes chapter. In the play of the senses of spring and summer, the beauty of the senses' revelation plays a role in educating the soul to wonder and to a feeling of communion with the cosmos. The themes of the recognition of external beauty and the soul's capacity to surrender in wonder form the backdrop to the expansion toward cosmic light and cosmic warmth.

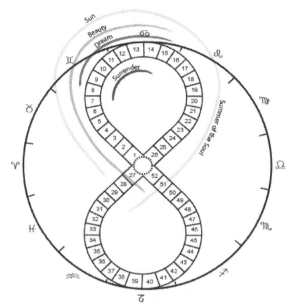

Figure 10: Spring/Summer Themes in the Calendar of the Soul

Closely allied to the two themes is a continuing dialogue with distinctive voices that speak in the verses from either the cosmos or the soul. Other voices appear throughout the year, particularly in the Spring Equinox quadrant, but the time of the Summer Solstice finds a majority of these (Figure 10).

Beauty

Beauty is expressed as such in the calendar (verses 52, 11, 12), or in terms of senses' glory (7), majesty (10), senses' revelation (14), and outer glory (15). It enters the world of the calendar during Holy Week, just before Easter (verse 52):

> When from the depths of soul
> The spirit turns to the life of worlds
> And beauty wells from wide expanses,

Then out of heaven's distances
Streams life-strength into human bodies,
Uniting by its mighty energy
The spirit's being with our human life.

Here beauty is perceived in the active effort of the spirit to turn to the life of worlds; it is offered in reply to it. The beauty that is offered in 52 is met from within by "gladness from the depths of soul" at Easter (verse 1):

When out of world-wide spaces
The sun speaks to the human mind,
And gladness from the depths of soul
Becomes, in seeing, one with light . . .

The sun of Christ allows us to reverse temporarily and dimly the course of nature, to go beyond the illusion of the senses, and to strengthen our etheric with that power of the spirit which is reflected at the senses' boundaries, but only if we bring our share of "gladness from the depths of soul."

This is closely followed in verse 2 by the fading of thinking's power ("the power of thinking loses self-confines"). The theme is continued with the soul's effort of overcoming the fetters and narrow bounds of selfhood (verses 3, 5, and 6). Wonder is the force that the soul calls forth in order to forget oneself (see "self-forgetfulness" of verse 3). Verse 7 calls our attention to the senses' glory:

My self is threatening to fly forth
Lured strongly by the world's enticing light.
Come forth, prophetic feeling,
Take up with strength your rightful task:
Replace in me the power of thought
Which in the senses' glory
Would ever lose itself.

Boding/intuition is that power which keeps us anchored to the depths of our being when everything in nature calls us outwardly. The self must strengthen itself before losing itself in the light and the macrocosm, just before the Whitsun impulse (verse 8) that individualizes.

We enter here the mid-season quadrant of the Summer Solstice (7 to 20). Intuition is now ascending and guiding the human soul toward receptivity to the cosmic Word. In the verses that follow, the soul actively gives itself to cosmic light and cosmic warmth, willingly sacrificing itself, and intuiting its union with the realm of the cosmic Word (verse 10). Beauty appears here in relation to "radiant heights" and "shining majesty":

To summer's radiant heights
The sun in shining majesty ascends;
It takes my human feeling
Into its own wide realms of space.
Within my inner being stirs
Presentiment which heralds dimly,
You shall in future know:
A godly being now has touched you.

Beauty, accompanied by enlivened feeling, further supports intuition in its effort to recognize the divine presence that illumines the soul. Verse 11 brings together the idea of surrendering to the beauty of the world and losing oneself to find oneself within the cosmic I:

In this the sun's high hour it rests
With you to understand these words of wisdom:
Surrendered to the beauty of the world,
Be stirred with new-enlivened feeling;
The human I can lose itself
And find itself within the cosmic I

The soul, filled with devotion and gratitude, recognizes itself surrounded by the power of the divine. It can experience the desire to soar to the cosmos to its true being and self and leave behind what is unworthy. Intuition has brought to birth "new-enlivened feeling," an echo and enhancement of perceptive feeling in 4. Beauty and the sense of wonder clearly facilitate the soul's capacity to surrender. The movement of surrender to cosmic light and cosmic warmth culminates in the yet unconscious receiving of cosmic Word, which will only reveal itself in verse 17.

Verse 12 amplifies 11. It is because we have been receptive to it that beauty can lead us even further:

> The radiant beauty of the world
> Compels my inmost soul to free
> God-given powers of my nature
> That they may soar into the cosmos,
> To take wing from my Self
> And trustingly to seek myself
> In cosmic light and cosmic warmth.

Verse 12 consumes the soul's desire to purify and sacrifice itself without full knowledge, in trust of what is to come; to experience powerlessness in order to let new powers emerge. This makes room in verses 13 and 14 to "the gods' own word of truth" and to cosmic thinking. In verse 15 beauty appears as outer glory:

> I feel enchanted weaving
> Of spirit within outer glory.
> In dullness of the senses
> It has enwrapt my being
> In order to bestow the strength
> Which in its narrow bounds my I
> Is powerless to give itself.

Here the movement of the soul takes a step forward. Beauty becomes "enchanted weaving of spirit within outer glory," and it is closely mentioned in relation to overcoming our narrow bounds in order to bestow true strength to the Self. Beauty is closely allied with surrender and seeking oneself in cosmic light and cosmic warmth, to which we turn next.

Surrender and Losing of Self

The threshold verse 7, which we quoted above, starts the surrender of the power of thinking. This is restated by thinking needing to rest content in quiet dream life in 8. Verse 9 asks that I "lose myself in light" and "lose yourself to find yourself":

> When I forget the narrow will of self,
> The cosmic warmth that heralds summer's glory
> Fills all my soul and spirit;
> To lose myself in light
> Is the command of spirit vision
> And intuition tells me strongly:
> O lose yourself to find yourself.

Cosmic warmth is the bridge between the sense world and the spirit world, made possible when I want to purify my lower ego. Warmth of the ego (enthusiasm) and cosmic warmth allow me to overcome the "narrow will of self." In the verse we find gathered beauty (summer's glory) and surrender with the theme that initiated both: "forgetting the narrow will of self."

Verse 11, quoted above, links the two themes again. It asks us to "surrender to the beauty of the world." Verse 12 continues and deepens this movement through the request of deeper inner activity by asking us to "free God-given powers of my nature" and

> . . . To take wing from myself
> And trustingly to seek myself
> In cosmic light and cosmic warmth.

The human being seeks beyond himself in trust toward cosmic light and cosmic warmth. Here surrender is equivalent to a movement of dying and becoming. The self wants to overcome its fetters, and when this is imbued with wonder, it can accomplish its ultimate sacrifice of taking wing from itself. Verse 13 continues by asking us to "seek expectantly to find our spirit kinship in spirit grounds." Verse 14 brings the movement to a close:

Surrendering to senses' revelation
I lost the drive of my own being,
And dreamlike thinking seemed
To daze and rob me of myself.
Yet quickening there draws near
In sense appearance cosmic thinking.

The first four lines of verse 14 recapitulate the path from Easter to St. John, but seen from the perspective of the ego, made to feel powerless. This powerlessness is the precondition for the in-streaming of cosmic thinking. It is through this willingness to relinquish control that the soul can be fertilized from outside. It can open itself to cosmic thinking, to the hierarchies thinking in us. In 15 this new birth is helped by "enchanted weaving of spirit within outer glory" enwrapping the Self in a protective gesture.

Our recognition of beauty and our willingness to surrender, trust, and expand into the cosmic light and cosmic warmth allow us to overcome our narrow boundaries of self. In this the movement from thinking to boding/intuition is essential. It becomes the compass of our inner world so that we don't lose ourselves in the natural movement of expansion.

Notice also that the culmination occurs in the descending part of the summer. We don't go out in ecstasy but are turned inward through the power of intuition that puts us in touch with cosmic thinking, with the cosmic intelligence. The recognition of beauty and the willingness to surrender ourselves to the forces of the cosmos, without losing ourselves, forms the prelude for the possibility of living the second part of the earth's out-breathing (after verse 15) inwardly.

Intuition and Voices in the Midsummer Quadrant

A closer look at the verses around the Summer Solstice reveals a dynamic of call and response; an interplay of speaking and listening. The speaking is done by the cosmos around us, or by the soul. Intuition is that faculty which is expressed at turns through listening, at others through steps the human being needs to take, suggested or indicated as necessity and even "command." We shall follow below the sequence of voices and the deeds of the soul that they call forth.

In verse 8 of Whitsun, the soul resolves to let human thinking rest content in a state of dream. We enter a period of dream that is similar to original participation, the condition of the human being in the original paradise, before the Fall. Intuition/boding will be our inward organ of sight. Verses 8 to 20 articulate the resolves taken from the inner voice of intuition, and these resolves are in living dialogue with the gifts received from cosmic light, cosmic warmth, and ultimately cosmic Word.

In verse 9, seen above, it is the inner voice of boding/intuition speaking. Through it we resolve to forget the narrow will of self and to lose ourselves in light. It is the warmth of the ego dedicated to its task that creates the bridge to cosmic warmth, and allows us to forget the narrow will of self.

In verse 10 the sun responds by taking human feeling into the wide realms of space in an echo to verse 4:

To summer's radiant heights
The sun in shining majesty ascends;
It takes my human feeling
Into its own wide realms of space.
Within my inner being stirs
Presentiment [intuition] which heralds dimly,
You shall in future know:
A godly being now has touched you.

The answer as to who this godly being is appears in verse 17, the mirror verse, as cosmic Word. The realm of the cosmic Word is first experienced in the greatest expansion of the soul, but dimly, after it has been willing to let go of the limitations of the personality. Now it is words of wisdom that speak within the soul in verse 11 (already mentioned above):

In this the sun's high hour it rests
With you to understand these words of wisdom:
Surrendered to the beauty of the world,
Be stirred with new-enlivened feeling;

The human I can lose itself
And find itself within the cosmic I.

Verse 11 echoes verse 9, which asks the soul to find itself in the cosmic light. The verse leads it a step further toward cosmic I. In the following verse we are asked to free our powers into the cosmos and seek ourselves in cosmic light and cosmic warmth. In verse 13 it is the gods' own word of truth, reminding us of cosmic Word, which speaks to the soul:

And when I live in senses' heights,
There flames up deep within my soul
Out of the spirit's fiery worlds
The gods' own word of truth:
In spirit sources seek expectantly [Seek through your boding power]
To find your spirit kinship.

The realm of the cosmic Word is indicated by the spirit's fiery worlds flaming in the soul and the gods' own word of truth. In verse 14 there draws near cosmic thinking in place of dreamlike thinking. In verse 15 we are enwrapped by enchanted weaving of spirit within outer glory. At the height of summer we are fully in a state of dream but conversing with the inner voice and light of intuition. This is done in order to receive and bestow strength. In verse 16 prophetic feeling imparts the stern command to "bear in inward keeping spirit bounty" for seeking "the fruits of selfhood."

In verse 17 the cosmic Word speaks, this time more explicitly: "imbue your spirit depths with my wide world-horizons."

Thus speaks the cosmic Word
That I by grace through senses' portals
Have led into my innermost soul:
Imbue your spirit depths
With my wide world horizons
To find in future time myself in you.

The spirit depths are that part of our being connected with cosmic life, our unconscious will. In response, in verse 18 I ask myself to expand my soul and to fashion it worthily as fitting raiment for the spirit. In verse 19 we have to encompass with memory what we have received, because it only lives in the depths of our being and has to be brought closer to the surface of consciousness. We are awakening from the dream that was inaugurated in verse 8. The end goal is that of awakening "ever strengthening selfhood forces" that will "give me to myself." In the same verse memory is called forth to move us away from a state of dream and awaken to the call of the fall.

The verses of the Summer Solstice quadrant alternate between the voice of boding (8, 9, 11, 12, 16, 18, 19) and the responses from the cosmos (10, 14, 15); between a voice speaking (9, 10, 11, 13, 17) and intuition requesting something of us (12, 16, 18, 19), if not both at the same time.

The cycle culminating into midsummer is one of entrusting ourselves to the dream and awakening to full consciousness through memory. Intuition guides us through the dream and acts as an inner voice, either explicit or implicit. When the soul does not speak as a voice, it speaks as suggestion and/or inner command asking something of us. To each voice that speaks follows a necessary action on the part of the soul. Intuition is that force that listens to the cosmos and the voices that call us from the future in order to die and become.

The whole culminates in verse 20 with the conscious decision to link our own life's reality with the world's existence, our lower self to the higher self. What was a dream in verse 8 (thinking weighed down to dreamlike dullness) becomes conscious striving (calling to memory) in 19.

Cosmic Word

Verses with reference to the cosmic Word appear at the height of summer and at the height of winter, and yet in very different and complementary ways.

From the beginning the polarity summer/winter appears. The true cosmic Word verses appear toward the end at midsummer (after midsummer), toward the beginning at midwinter (before midwinter). In other, previous summer verses, cosmic Word received subconsciously is not stated but implied.

In verse 8 the first mention is that of "godly being" desiring "union with my soul." In verse 10 my "human feeling" is taken by the sun "to summer's radiant heights" where I intuit "a godly being now has touched you." This is the cosmic Word, as it will be revealed in verse 17, mirror verse of 10, which explicitly mentions it.

In verse 11 the human I finds itself in the cosmic I. In verse 13 the "god's own word of truth" speaks "out of the spirit's fiery worlds" asking me to "seek expectantly spirit kinship in spirit grounds." This is followed by the approach of cosmic thinking in verse 14, which wants to read us like a letter in the alphabet of the Word. We can surrender in order to be inspired and to willingly play a role in earth evolution. This has been the object of the whole containment of the self during the summer.

After being "enwrapped in enchanted weaving of spirit" (15) the cosmic Word emerges as such in verses 17 and 18. In verse 17 the cosmic Word asks that we expand our views in our spirit depths through its "wide world-horizons." In verse 18 it is the human being who asks himself how he can expand his soul to unite with cosmic Word:

> Can I expand my soul
> That it unites itself
> With cosmic Word received as seed?
> I sense [I do forebode] that I must find the strength
> To fashion worthily my soul
> As fitting raiment fort the spirit.

The whole reaches a climax in verse 19 when the soul can look back through memory at the experience of the summer in order to render it conscious and nurture the fruits of selfhood growing in its womb.

Spring and Summer: Letting Go, Letting Come, and Letting Grow

It is worth noticing the dynamic movement between verses 7 to 13 on one hand and verses 14 to 20 on the other.

An active movement of surrender is requested in verses 9, 11, 12 (lose yourself) and again in 12 (God-given powers to soar into the cosmos). In response to verse 11's generic words of wisdom that enjoin that the "human I can lose itself and find itself in the cosmic I," in 12 we are no longer asked to lose ourselves but to "seek" ourselves in cosmic light and cosmic warmth. We now hear the gods' own word of truth, no longer to lose but to find spirit kinship as a culmination in verse 13. As König would have us notice, we have moved from losing to seeking and finding.

Verse 14 is the one called "Summer verse" even though it is in July (7 to 13), showing that the culmination of St. John's festival happens after St. John. We start now a new series of 13 verses, and these are ushered in by cosmic thinking in 14. We are no longer seeking but receiving from the cosmos. In response the cosmos strengthens us through enchanted weaving that enwraps us in 15. Verse 15 reminds us of the narrow bounds of self, referred to in the spring, but shows us that they can be overcome. It's the last time that they are mentioned.

When we awaken from the enchanted weaving, we are no longer seeking outwardly (cosmic light, cosmic warmth) but cultivating inwardly what has been received. Likewise, intuition directs us no longer outwardly but inwardly. The crowning of intuition's efforts is the emergence of selfhood in 19, 21, and 22. In verse 19 is announced that "selfhood's forces shall be awakened from within . . . and give me to myself." Then in 20 comes the warning verse, and the theme of selfhood emerges.

In summing up, in the spring we confront the reality of narrowness of self (fetters of selfhood in 3, narrow selfhood's inner power in 5, narrow limits in 6, narrow will of self in 9). Intuition emerges in full force in 7 asking us to sacrifice the narrow will of self and to seek cosmic light and cosmic warmth. To the letting go of verses 7 to 13 correspond the "letting come" and "letting grow" of verses 14 to 19. The climax is reached in 19 with the inner discovery of "ever strengthening, selfhood's forces" that will "give me to myself." Yes, this is the time of new challenge, but the soul now has everything it needs, down to a new, emerging budding selfhood. All it needs to do is emerge from midsummer's dream through a conscious effort of recollection, demanded in verse 19. New themes emerge after the warning verse 20.

What Does St. John Request of Us?

In the summer the human being is drawn out of herself, her consciousness expanded, though she has to struggle to retain what amounts to flashes of intuition, and refrain from losing herself in a sort of undifferentiated cosmic consciousness. We are meeting the cosmic intelligence, but we have to find an inner compass through which not to lose ourselves in the stimulation of the senses and in a falsely expanded, dreamy consciousness. Intuition becomes our inner compass and light. Through it we can become conscious instruments of the cosmic intelligence.

From the weaving of the various themes above we can realize that the time of the Summer Solstice is one of looking back on one hand, but of listening to the future on the other. This meeting of the streams of time—one from the past, the other from the future—is the essence itself of the historical and moral consciousness that the archangel Uriel imparts at midsummer. It is through this historical consciousness that we understand how we have to transform and overcome the "narrow will of self," the shortcomings that we have to let go of, or change in ourselves, in order that better futures may come to us and come to be. At St. John we know that the Baptist asks us that Christ increase in us and that we decrease. This is reflected in the curbing of the lower self so methodically pursued in the verses leading to St. John and shortly after.

As Emil Bock proposes, the whole pre-Christian gesture of ecstasy has to be changed, and the time of St. John is really more extended than the festival itself.[29]

In verses 14 and 15 we see what this gesture can be: one of containment and listening within, isolated from the frenzy of the external world.

St. John should be seen as a season, not just a day; it is a preparation for the descent toward fall. It should go from the day of maximum expansion to the time of contraction. St. John will be the festival of the growth of Christ in us. After the festival the Earth starts in-breathing, and this corresponds to the fact that we must turn inward and let the Christ in us grow through an appeasement of the external fever of activity that accompanies summer.

---

[29] Emil Bock, *The Circle of the Year's Festivals: A Collection of Essays*. See essay "From the Pagan Solstice Festival to the Christian Festival of Saint John."

As Emil Bock suggests, at St. John the old fires of ecstasy must be replaced by the fires of sacrifice. This is why at present we don't celebrate at the solstice but three days later. In future we should celebrate on the following Sunday, just as we do at Easter. In both instances we should wait to celebrate after nature's extremes.

CHAPTER 5

WINTER SOLSTICE THEMES

We will now look at the time of the Winter Solstice—chiefly at the verses 33 to 46—and the themes that are woven around it, in contrast to the time of the Summer Solstice. We will anchor this time of the year around the Christmas imagination that Rudolf Steiner offered us in the year 1923.

The Christmas Imagination

In winter the elemental beings have been in-breathed into the earth and are most intimately united with it, and the earth is most self-contained. The earth now consists most of all of salt processes. The mercury process (prevalent in the spring) is still visible in the tendency to assume a spherical shape in the snow cover; the sulphur process is not active. Within the surface of the earth we also find the result of the accumulation of the ash-process (result of combustion/sulphur processes of the summer) through the fall of seeds, petals, pollen, and so forth. From the fall the Earth is as if impregnated by the ash, which activates an "ash-forming process."

The working together of the mercury and salt processes bring forth and activate a general quickening of the Earth's capacity to produce new life. If it were only for the salt process the new life would become Moon-life; this is countered by the presence of ash through which the Moon-like is led back into the earthly.

In the spheres above, the Sun radiates warmth into the air and light.

This warmth, working in the air, transforms Earth-activity into cosmic activity. As a result our thinking faculty is turned away from the immediate concerns of the Earth. It acquires a certain lightness and flexibility.

The salt/Moon-forming activities are stronger in woman than in man. "The woman becomes Moon, just as the Earth—especially just below its surface—becomes Moon when Christmas approaches."[30] The formation of the new human being, however, stands under the influence of the Sun. This is the time of the year in which Christmas is meant to happen, and Mary, whose "head reflects something heavenly in its whole appearance"[31] prepares to take the Sun into herself and give birth to the child in the Moon-earthly element.

Further above the initiate can see the imprint of the human heads of the souls pressing for incarnation. Steiner concludes: "The only possible way of presenting [Mary] is in this form: with the Moon-forces below, with the Sun forces in the middle, and above, toward the head, with the forces of the stars. The picture of Mary with the little Jesus-child arises out of the cosmos itself."[32]

In old times conception could only take place in spring, before the human being was emancipated from this necessity by Lucifer. Even at present the children who approach incarnation do so at the time of the end of winter, even if they will be born later on during the year.

The time of the Holy Nights deserves a special mention in relation to the whole of winter. This is a time in which the plant kingdom merges in consciousness with the mineral world of the Earth and its processes. The two states of consciousness merge and interpenetrate. At the time of the Holy Nights the plant kingdom "becomes aware of the secrets of the stars and uses them, so that in the springtime the plants may unfold again and bear blossoms and fruits in accordance with the mysteries of the cosmos."[33] When the human being communes with the consciousness of the plant

---

[30] Rudolf Steiner, *Four Seasons and the Archangels*, lecture 2 of October 6, 1923.

[31] Rudolf Steiner, *Four Seasons and the Archangels*, lecture 2 of October 6, 1923.

[32] Rudolf Steiner, *Four Seasons and the Archangels*, lecture 2 of October 6, 1923.

[33] Rudolf Steiner, *The Year's Course as a Symbol for the Great Cosmic Year*, lecture of December 31, 1915.

kingdom, then he can extend his consciousness a little like Olav Åsteson did during this time of the year.[34]

The winter half of the year is ushered in by Micha-el. Whereas the summer time of the year is associated with historical events in the life of Christ and the life of nature, the winter opens us up to the striving of the inner life in connection to the hierarchies.

Micha-el is the countenance of the Christ and of the hierarchies; he prepares himself to be the countenance of humanity. At this time of the year, the world of the hierarchies must replace the natural kingdoms in the life of the human being.

Micha-el teaches us the principle of openness to the above. All hierarchies are part of a continuum that is open to what is higher; so must the human being be. Lucifer forewent this openness, and so does the human being who does not look at the gesture and invitation of Micha-el. When we let him work in our soul, Micha-el turns us toward the future and activates our will.

As we have done in relation to the Summer Solstice, we will turn to the themes that offer us an understanding of the winter part of the year. We will turn to hope, the meaning of life and destiny, continued in the themes of heart, warmth, and love, before turning to the central theme of the cosmic Word and of the "spirit-birth" that culminates around Christmas (Figure 11).

---

[34] See *Olaf Åsteson: The Awakening of the Earth Spirit*, lecture of January 7, 1913.

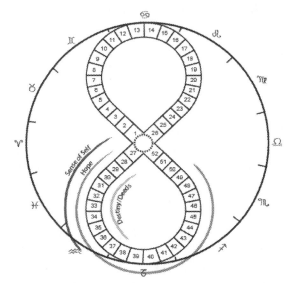

Figure 11: Themes in the Winter Quadrant of the Year

Hope

At the beginning of fall, hope is wishfulness that lames; it appears in verse 28:

I can, in newly quickened inner life,
Sense wide horizons in myself.
The force and radiance of my thought—
Coming from soul's sun power—
Can solve the mysteries of life,
And grant fulfilment now to wishes
Whose wings have long been lamed by hope.

Verses 27 and 28 mark an important transition. Verse 27 is the last verse in which intuition carries its effort from the summer. It contemplates the Self as a gift of the summer sun and a germinating seed. Now the light-filled gesture of intuition, last met in 21 (light-filled expectation), is carried in the Self as gift of the summer sun and becomes "radiance of thought coming from soul's Sun power." Intuition has been carrying the Self in the light and passed on the baton to thinking, itself a gift of the light.

The theme of the will left lame is brought to a completion in the next verse. In 29 it is once more the spark of thinking, become a flame, that will nourish my winter hope:

> To fan the spark of thinking into flame
> By my own strong endeavor,
> To read life's inner meaning
> Out of the cosmic spirit's fount of strength:
> This is my summer heritage,
> My autumn solace, and my winter hope.

But it is also the cosmic spirit's fount of strength that will closely support it, as the verse specifies in "to read life's inner meaning out of the cosmic spirit's fount of strength." Wisdom and strength carry true hope through the winter.

The power of the cosmic Word rises to a pitch in verses 36 to 38, and in 38 it begets "the heavenly fruit of hope in my soul's core." Through thinking the cosmic Word becomes conscious of itself in 38 (Christmas) and hope becomes the "heavenly fruit of hope":

> The spirit child within my soul
> I feel freed of enchantment.
> In heart-high gladness has
> The holy cosmic Word engendered
> The heavenly fruit of hope,
> Which grows rejoicing into worlds afar
> Out of my being's godly roots.

The winter hope of 29 becomes a reality not just for the Self but for the world. At the end of winter, in verse 49 (beginning of Passiontide), where hope appears for the fourth time, it is once more my clarity of thought that turns its rays of hope to the coming cosmic day:

> I feel the force of cosmic life:
> Thus speaks my clarity of thought,
> Recalling its own spirit growth
> Through nights of cosmic darkness,

And to the new approach of cosmic day
It turns its inward rays of hope.

Again hope is associated with the power of thinking in its sunlike quality. It looks to the future. The sun of thinking recognizes the sun of nature. During the summer youthful hope grows old, and this is reflected at the beginning of fall in verse 28's "wishes whose wings have long been lamed by hope."

Note that the two verses complementary to 28 and 29 are 24 and 25 and they speak of the darkness of the soul, and of space and time: verse 24, "from the darkness of the soul creates the fruit of self-engendered will"; verse 25, "into the dark of space and time. Toward sleep is urging all creation." In contrast to the darkness, hope emerges from the Michaelic will and the sunlike quality of thinking.

In the 1911 lectures on faith, love, and hope, Rudolf Steiner associates hope with the physical body (body of hope), faith with the with the astral body, and love with the etheric. And hope manifests in the calendar when the earth is at its most mineral/physical state in winter. König indicates that hope is what we can cultivate most firmly through the knowledge of the reality of karma and reincarnation.

Meaning of Life, Destiny, and Deeds

The self is emerging to knowledge of itself in verses 24 to 27. After this the verses that concern us occupy the span going from 28 to 36.

In verse 28, just mentioned, the "radiance of thought" helps us "solve the mysteries of life." Verse 29 is pivotal: it enjoins us to "read life's inner meaning out of the cosmic spirit's fount of strength," uniting wisdom and strength. In verse 31 "forceful will of life" wants to manifest itself in "creative powers soul-impelled to ripen into human deeds:"

The light from spirit depths
Strives to ray outwards, sun-imbued;
Transformed to forceful will of life
It shines into the senses' dullness
To bring to birth the powers

Whereby creative powers, soul-impelled,
Shall ripen into human deeds.

Verse 32 renders this intent even more conscious:

I feel my own force, bearing fruit
And gaining strength to give me to the world.
My inmost being I feel charged with power
To turn with clearer insight
Toward the weaving of life's destiny.

Gaining a deeper understanding of the forces of destiny was already announced in verse 28 ("read life's inner meaning"); here it gains in depth and precision, and it informs our deeds. After the threshold verse (33) the motif reappears twice again, the first time in verse 34:

In secret inwardly to feel
How all that I've preserved of old
Is quickened by new-risen sense of self:
This shall, awakening, pour forth cosmic forces
Into the outer actions of my life
And, in growing, mould me into true existence.

Here we notice that it is through the connection to our higher self (sense of self) that we can move toward seeking the blessing and the help of the spiritual world in our deeds. The next verse specifies in which direction this enhancement can occur:

Can I know life's reality
So that it's found again
Within my soul's creative urge?
I feel that I am granted power
To make my Self, as humble part,
At home within the cosmic Self.

The urge toward "life's reality" in verse 35 is an enhancement of verses 31 and 32 because now I want to "make the Self at home within the cosmic

Self." In other words, I want to act out of the forces of the Spirit Self. Having met the cosmic Self we reach a culmination of the theme when the cosmic Word asks me to "imbue my labor's aims with [its] bright spirit light to sacrifice myself through [Him]" in verse 36:

> Within my being's depths there speaks,
> Intent on revelation,
> The cosmic Word mysteriously:
> Imbue your labor's aims
> With my bright spirit light
> To sacrifice yourself through me.

The verses indicate an alignment of our will with the cosmic will, a way of acting in the world strengthened by a clearer understanding of the forces of destiny and a fuller sense of being. Aligning with the cosmic will ultimately means being willing to sacrifice oneself.

At this point the theme of destiny and its forces fades away, but another one emerges soon after and is closely connected with the first: the forces of the heart, warmth, and love. In verse 36 something important appears in the soul being asked to sacrifice itself through the power of the cosmic Word. The cosmic Word, which comes in strength in verses 36 to 38, forms the bridge to the following theme.

Heart, Warmth, and Love

As soon as we break off with the meaning of life/destiny verse, from 37 onward we have a theme interweaving heart, warmth, and love, most clearly in verses 37, 38, 40, 41, 42, 43, and 48.

It is not a coincidence that verses 36 and 37 herald the arrival of cosmic Word. In 37 the heart, mentioned for the first time, is impelled "to carry spirit light into world winter night"

> To carry spirit light into world-winter-night
> My heart is ardently impelled,
> That shining seeds of soul
> Take root in grounds of worlds

And Word Divine through senses' darkness
Resounds, transfiguring all life.

The Christmas verse comes in joyful response to the presence of cosmic Word that has carried its seeds since the time of St. John:

The spirit child within my soul
I feel freed of enchantment.
In heart-high gladness has
The holy cosmic Word engendered
The heavenly fruit of hope,
Which grows rejoicing into worlds afar
Out of my being's godly roots.

After the Christmas verse of the spirit-birth through the cosmic Word, the human soul gains its place as co-creator, no matter how small, in the order of creation. Now its deeds can have world-forming effects because they can let the cosmic Word shine through its being.

It is not surprising that after verse 38 the theme we explore goes to a crescendo. In the next verse the power of thinking frees in the soul the sense of Self. We will now see the heart/warmth theme appear in four consecutive verses. In verse 40 the "fiery power of the cosmic Word" acquires a cleansing capacity:

And when I live in spirit depths
And dwell within my soul's foundations,
There streams from love-worlds of the heart,
To fill the vain delusion of the self,
The fiery power of the cosmic Word.

We can take note in passing that the expression "love-worlds of the heart" corresponds in the complementary verse 13 to "spirit's fiery worlds." It is as if these fiery worlds appear now within the human being, in her heart. Verse 41 sounds:

The soul's creative might
Strives outward from the heart's own core

To kindle and inflame god-given powers
In human life to right activity;
The soul thus shapes itself
In human loving and in human working.

Through words like "kindle" and "inflame," the verse confirms that
we are working out of the cosmic warmth region of the cosmic Word. It
reaffirms the place of the heart and introduces the idea that deeds impelled
from the heart have for motivation and object human loving. The cosmic
Word can bring us warmth and unshakeable certainty in the middle of
winter as in the following, verse 42:

In this the shrouding gloom of winter
The soul feels ardently impelled
To manifest its innate strength,
To guide itself to realms of darkness,
Anticipating thus
Through warmth of heart the sense-world's revelation.

In this verse we are already looking to and preparing for the incoming
expression of the external joy of growth. The permeation of the human
being through the forces of the cosmic Word and the redeeming power
of a metamorphosed thinking are expressed in the coming two verses:
warmth and forces of the heart in 43, soul clarity and spirit-birth in 44.
Verse 43 reads:

In winter's depths is kindled
True spirit life with glowing warmth;
It gives to world appearance,
Through forces of the heart, the power to be.
Grown strong, the human soul defies
With inner fire the coldness of the world.

Here, in the verse that completes the quartet, the themes we have been
exploring are brought together; glowing warmth, forces of the heart, and
inner fire. Love is implied.

Verses 44 to 47 occupy us with the strengthening of the power of thinking and remind us of the spirit-birth. In between appears the threshold verse 46 indicating the danger of the coming strength of the world of the senses overwhelming the forces of the soul. Our theme is brought to a conclusion in verse 48 when thinking itself is crowned by cosmic thinking attained in the human being, no longer a gift of the Gods, as it was in the summer:

> Within the light that out of world-wide heights
> Would stream with power toward the soul,
> May certainty of cosmic thinking
> Arise to solve the soul's engimas—
> And focusing its mighty rays,
> Awaken love in human hearts.

Love and knowledge are married in what amounts to a verse of celebration.

Cosmic Word and Spirit-Birth

Thinking starts to ascend in verses 28 to 30. Verses 31 and 32 have strong elements of will. This expresses itself in forceful will of life and in the desire to be of service to the world. The theme of finding amplifies from verses 33 to 36. In 33 (threshold verse) resounds the threat of the world finding only death if it cannot re-create itself in human souls. In verse 34 emerges the sense of self that wants to "pour forth cosmic forces into the outer actions of my life." This becomes yearning "to know what it is 'to be'" and for "life's reality ... within my soul's creative urge." The self wants to make itself at home within the cosmic Self. This deep yearning creates the entryway for the cosmic Word in the soul in verses 36 to 38.

Verse 36 answers all the yearnings that have emerged in verses 27 to 35, especially verses 34 and 35, which express the desire for true existence and true life. It reads:

> Within my being's depths there speaks,
> Intent on revelation,
> The cosmic Word mysteriously:

Imbue your labor's aims
With my bright spirit light
To sacrifice yourself through me.

Notice here that in this verse appears the only voice that speaks in the winter, that of cosmic Word. Verse 37, mentioned above, responds to the human being's determination to carry light into the darkness of winter. Through him can cosmic Word resound in and transform the world.

Verse 38 of Christmas is pivotal in weaving together various themes and introducing a new one:

The spirit child within my soul
I feel freed of enchantment.
In heart-high gladness has
The holy cosmic Word engendered
The heavenly fruit of hope,
Which grows rejoicing into worlds afar
Out of my being's godly roots.

Verse 38 is the complementary of mid-July verse 15 in which the "enchanted weaving of spirit within outer glory" has "enwrapt my being." Now the veil has fallen and cosmic Word is manifest. The chrysalis enveloped in the cocoon has emerged and given birth to the resurrected butterfly. Cosmic Word has taken residence in the soul, and this is what is expressed with the term "spirit-birth." From this moment we can follow the two themes.

Cosmic Word reappears in verse 39 with a cleansing effect on the "vain delusions of self." Spirit-birth means that a new being is born in the soul, who renews the vow to sacrifice himself through cosmic Word of verse 36.

Verses 40 to 43 form what we have called the quartet of the heart. Spirit-birth appears in the pivotal verses 44 and 45, just before the threshold verse. The challenge of verse 43 comes in the preparation for the growth of cosmic life and the effect it has on our life of the senses, the danger of the separation of the soul forces. This can be forestalled if thinking fortifies itself and transforms itself in order to recognize the formative forces active in nature, to which it is akin. Verse 44 states:

In reaching for new sense attractions,
Soul-clarity would fill,
Mindful of spirit-birth attained,
The world's bewildering, sprouting growth
With the creative will of my own thinking.

The world will not engulf us if we can meet it equipped with a metamorphosed thinking; the will of this thinking is of the same nature as that of the bewildering sprouting growth. This prepares us for meeting the world's becoming in the right soul mood in verse 45:

My power of thought grows firm
United with the spirit's birth.
It lifts the senses' dull attractions
To bright-lit clarity.
When soul-abundance
Desires union with the world's becoming,
Must senses' revelation
Receive the light of thinking.

Cosmic Word in the Cosmos and in the Human Being

The realm of cosmic Word is expressed in words of great beauty in Lesson 19 of the First Class of the School of Spiritual Science in ways that people familiar with the Calendar of the Soul will clearly recognize in its structure. After all, the calendar owes its existence to the Spirits of the Cycles of Time in the realm of the cosmic Word, and this is the realm addressed in the lesson, given in full below:

The human I knows it is [in] the realm of the Spirit Word
sustained by the Serpahim, Cherubim and Thrones

The Guardian speaks from afar
Who speaks in the Spirit-Word
With the voice
That glows in the Fire of Worlds?

From the realm of the First Hierarchy
There speaks the Flames of the Stars,
There flame Seraphinian Powers of Fire
In my heart too they are aflame.
In the eternal Fount of Love
Human heart shall find
Speech of the Spirit Flames creating
It is I.

The Guardian speaks from afar
What thinks in the Spirit-Word
With the thoughts
That build from the Souls of Worlds?

From the realm of the First Hierarchy
There think the Lights of the Stars,
There light the Cherubims' building forces
In my head too their light shines forth.
In the eternal Fount of Light
Human head shall find
Thought of the building of souls e'er working
It is I.

The Guardian speaks from afar
What wields strength in the Spirit-Word
With the forces
That live in the Body of Worlds.

From the realm of the First Hierarchy
There wields strength the Body of Worlds of Stars,
There body the Thrones' sustaining powers.
In my limbs too they body forth.
In the eternal Fount of Life
Human limbs shall find
Force of the Bearers of Worlds e'er wielding
It is I.

In the expressions "flames of the stars," "eternal fount of love," and "human heart"; "lights of the stars," "eternal fount of light," and "human head"; "body of the worlds of stars," "eternal fount of life," and "human limbs" do we not recognize the expressions of cosmic life, cosmic light, and cosmic warmth in the Calendar of the Soul? These are the forces at work behind the four ethers whose rhythmic interactions are made apparent in the course of the seasons.

In external nature, to the alternation of the seasons correspond the dynamic changing relationships between the ethers. In the spring the tone ether rises toward the light ether, and higher still toward the warmth ether as the year moves into summer. This is what lives behind the course of the seasons, the in-breathing and out-breathing of the Earth and its living beings.

Higher than the ethers we find the deeds of the cosmic Word and everything that issues from the realm of the First Hierarchy, from the realms of cosmic life, cosmic light, and cosmic warmth. What appears in the out-breathing of the Earth during the time of original participation of the warm part of the year returns via the human being in the in-breathing part of the year during fall and winter. Thus we can expect to see it metamorphosed. To form a link between the expression of cosmic Word in the ethers and in the human being. let us turn to insights that Steiner offers us in *The Cosmic Word and Individual Man*.[35]

When asleep the human physical body rests, but the etheric body becomes more active. The places where the organs of sense lay radiate inner light. Another process during sleep manifests in an inner humming and singing that fills the human being, leaving strong impressions on astral body and ego. Finally, from the surface of the skin inward, there are etheric streams of heat. It is these three streams that detach from the human being into the cosmic ether a few days after death.

These sources of light, sound, and warmth reveal the mighty workings of the Exusiai, or Spirits of Form. The three activities altogether give form to the etheric organism of the human being. Steiner comments, "If one contemplates this etheric organism with spiritual vision, . . . one is bound to describe it as consisting simply of the forms of thoughts, of flowing thoughts." And further: "It is the thought-process of the Universe

---

[35] Rudolf Steiner, *The Cosmic Word and Individual Man*, lecture of May 2, 1923.

individualized. This individualized thought-process of the Universe reveals itself as individualized Logos [cosmic Word]."[36]

The above thought processes speak silently something that can be perceived as belonging to the inner man. "It speaks indeed—as all things through the Logos [cosmic Word] speak to us—in an individual form, expressing in an inner Word, that can be perceived spiritually, the essential being of Man." And further: "Speech, which otherwise is directed outwards to the ears of our fellow men, is as if transformed, turned inwards etherically. It is as if we were to repeat everything which we have said during the day, from waking to falling asleep—but in the opposite order, beginning in the evening and ending with the morning . . . in a way that reveals the whole nature of our soul."[37] Behind this we find the activity of the Dynamis.

This picture is completed with mention of the etheric formation that is found opposite to the vertebral column, and that connects the streams of the astral body through the chakras, linking the ether body to the astral body. It is an expression of the work of the Kyriotetes. Thus the ether body is the conjoined working of Exusiai, Dynamis, and Kyriotetes.

Steiner goes on to speak about the beings of the First Hierarchy:

> Men knew that all these Beings . . . existed in the universe, and shine out, manifesting themselves, revealing themselves in speech. They knew that this expression in speech proceeded from their essential being. And that universal resounding which arises from the confluence of what is spoken by the particular Beings on self-revelation, this is the Logos. But to begin with, the Logos was also only an *appearance*. Only because Christ united this appearance, and made it concrete in His own Being, was through the Mystery of Golgotha the apparent Logos born upon earth as a real Logos.

In summer the cosmic Word is preceded by cosmic life, cosmic light,

---

[36] Rudolf Steiner, *The Cosmic Word and Individual Man*, lecture of May 2, 1923.
[37] Rudolf Steiner, *The Cosmic Word and Individual Man*, lecture of May 2, 1923.

cosmic warmth, and cosmic I. It creates a seed in our soul that we nurture to existence through the end of the summer.

In winter cosmic Word follows the emergence of the sense of Self and the solar power of thought. Cosmic life becomes Michaelic will, cosmic light becomes thinking, and cosmic warmth is commuted in forces of the heart. What occurred through the forces of the cosmos is now brought about by the human being himself. Some of the fall/winter verses exemplify these metamorphoses. In verse 26 of Michaelmas we hear: "O Nature, your maternal life I bear within the essence of my will." The inner relationship between cosmic light and thinking appears in many ways. Verse 30, as one of them, expresses "There flourish in the sunlight of my soul the ripened fruits of thinking." And, as for cosmic warmth we can offer the example of verse 40: "There streams from love-worlds of the heart . . . the fiery power of the cosmic Word." To follow more closely this movement of transformation see Appendix 3.

While the earth is most self-contained, the spirit-birth at Christmas is that of the spirit child that has the power to transmute the bleak reality of winter. The child that Mary bore historically becomes in us the birth of cosmic Word, nurtured by the sun-illumined new quality of thinking. We bring to birth this child of soul for the rejoicing of the world. We join the work of creation. To borrow Barfield's terminology, the original participation of the summer becomes conscious participation in the winter.

CHAPTER 6

EQUINOXES THEMES

B efore starting to look at the equinoxes' quadrants, we will turn to some considerations about the connection between the two festivals of Easter and Michaelmas.

Michaelmas as Easter in the Fall

Easter does not correspond to the pagan Spring Equinox festival of the rebirth of nature. Rather it is more closely connected with the Adonis festival of the God who was drowned into the waters of the sea and reemerged after three days, a celebration that took place in autumn. In effect the Mystery of the Resurrection can better be understood when the forces of nature are in decline and the human being has to turn to his own forces.

The purpose of the old pagan mysteries of the fall was to reveal the true meaning and purpose of death and the soul's ascent to the spiritual worlds. However, in approaching the time of Christ, human beings could no longer understand the mysteries of resurrection without the external help of the forces of nature and their regeneration.

In his lecture of April 12, 1924, Steiner indicates that for human beings the true Easter festival relates to the autumn time of Michaelmas; for nature, Easter takes place in the spring.[38] The time in which nature

---

[38] Rudolf Steiner, *The Easter Festival in the Evolution of the Mysteries*, lecture of April 19, 1924.

withdraws and dies away is the best time for human beings to ponder about their inner ascent and resurrection in the spirit. In the fall we can penetrate more consciously the forces of decline and death and awaken the spirit. And we can be fully reborn in the spirit at the time of Christmas.

The revelation of Micha-el can be consecrated at Christmas; Micha-el can lead us to the Christ. We awaken to the spirit at Michaelmas; the spirit is born in us at Christmas. The Michaelmas festival is what allows the human being to overcome the risk of the death of the spirit inherent to the time of the consciousness soul.

I. Spring and Easter

The Easter Imagination

In the winter season, in relation to limestone in the soil the initiate perceives a state of "inner contentment." As we come out of winter the limestone is as if dull in comparison to its winter state. While the elemental beings are gradually being breathed out of the earth, the limestone expresses an inner vitality and becomes full of desire, partly due to plants' activity and their intake of water and carbonic acid from the limestone. All of this attracts Ahrimanic beings to the limestone and tempts them to spread their presence all over nature. They try to bring down an "astral rain," and they fall into the yearly recurrent illusion that they can thus ensoul the Earth. But they achieve something else; the human being consumes the fruits of the earth that are produced in an atmosphere of hope and illusion, and in this way the Ahrimanic beings can reach the human being, whom they would like to dissolve within the Earth.

The Ahrimanic beings are of an etheric nature and would like to gain an astral sheath in the earth. Under their influence the human being would become like living limestone, calcify and turn into a sclerotic form with something like bat-like wings.

On the other hand the elemental beings are drawn into the region of air and cloud-formation, permeated by Luciferic beings. These beings are of a purely astral nature and would like to gain an etheric sheath for themselves. When the plants start drawing up the carbonic acid, this falls under the sphere of Lucifer.

If Lucifer were successful, human beings would lose the ability to breathe and all animal life would be extinguished. The Luciferic being would transform the human being in a body of earth-vapor but only as far down as the breast; they would give him cloud-like wings in front of which would form an enlarged larynx. "The Luciferic being grasps through his ear formation what he has sensed with his wings, and through the larynx—closely connected with the ear—this knowledge becomes the creative word that works and weaves in the forms of living beings."[39] If Lucifer were successful, he would unite the human etheric bodies with his astrality.

The combined result of Ahrimanic and Luciferic activities is what Steiner represented in his monumental sculptural group. At Easter the Mystery of Golgotha is renewed every year cosmically. Between the two adversaries, whose striving has been described above, is inserted the Christ, with Ahriman at his feet, and Lucifer held in check above him. At this time of the year is active the archangel Raphael; he shows the human being how much Ahriman and Lucifer will lead him to illness, and where to find the Christ healing principle. The limestone can be countered with the healing influence of everything of a salt-nature, and of the sulphurous, phosphoric element in the rising carbonic acid.

As we have done in the previous two chapters, we will now follow interrelated themes in the Easter quadrant that goes from verses 47 to 7 (Figure 12). Among these are the themes of cosmic life, of memory, and of the voices speaking in the quadrant.

---

[39] Rudolf Steiner, *Four Seasons and the Archangels*, lecture 3.

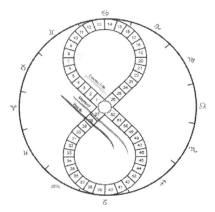

Figure 12: Themes in the Spring Equinox Quadrant

Cosmic Life

In looking at the theme we will divide the quadrant in the ascending section leading to Easter and the descending section after Easter.

Verses 47 to 52
The threshold verse 46 that precedes the quadrant speaks of spirit depths; and of inward sight which needs to be sustained through strength of will. Verse 47 already brings out the joy of growth that points to the emergence of the life and chemical ethers, and the powers that stand above them—cosmic life in the language of the calendar:

> There will arise out of the world's great womb,
> Quickening the senses' life, the joy of growth.
> Now may it find my strength of thought
> Well-armed by powers divine
> Which strongly live within my being.

In this verse the emerging element of life is met with the will present in thinking, and this is expressed emphatically, with "well-armed" and two expressions of strength. In verse 48 the theme of thinking of the previous mid-season quadrant (33 to 46) exhausts itself and is crowned in cosmic thinking, the power with which the human being can meet the emerging life of the senses without as yet losing himself in it. When Easter and the Christ Mystery approach, the soul's orientation will change again.

Verse 49 announces the deed of Golgotha and its effect on the human being. The sphere of cosmic life draws near:

I feel the force of cosmic life:
Thus speaks my clarity of thought,
Recalling its own spirit growth
Through nights of cosmic darkness,
And to the new approach of cosmic day
It turns its inward rays of hope.

Verse 50 brings together the joy of growth of 47 and cosmic life of 49:

Thus to the human ego speaks
In mighty revelation,
Unfolding its inherent powers,
The joy of growth throughout the world:
I carry into you my life
From its enchanted bondage
And so attain my true goal.

The life is enchanted because the realms of life ether and harmony of the spheres (sound ether) are no longer directly accessible to the human being; they become so only through the Christ. But cosmic life becomes accessible to the human being who has attained cosmic thinking. Now spirit worlds seek and find themselves in the human being.

Cosmic life now becomes cosmic spirit (Steiner also uses the term *cosmic ether*) in 51. The approaching of Easter (Holy Week, verse 52) offers an explosion of the forces of life:

When from the depths of soul
The spirit turns to the life of worlds
And beauty wells from wide expanses,
Then out of heaven's distances
Streams life-strength into human bodies,

99

Uniting by its mighty energy
The spirit's being with the life of man.

The sphere of the Christ draws near and brings the sphere of cosmic life closer to the human being.

Verses 1 to 7
In verse 1 it is the sun who, alone through the year, speaks at Easter:

When out of world-wide spaces
The sun speaks to the human mind,
And gladness from the depths of soul
Becomes, in seeing, one with light,
Then rising from the sheath of self,
Thoughts soar to distances of space
And dimly bind
The human being to the spirit's life.

The movement of union with cosmic life is completed, and its nature changed, when thoughts that the I has made its own dissolve, as it were in distances of space, but not without offering us a bridge to the realm of Christ, to the cosmic life.

In verse 2 appears a veiled warning. Yes, the spheres of the spirit have been seeking the realm of the human, and in response the human being is expanding his being in the highest ethers; yet this expansion can no longer occur through thinking, but through something that the human being must find within. The unique expression of "the World-All" appears in 3, reminding us of that original spiritual world in which humanity was joined as one, "in self-forgetfulness and mindful of its primal state" and in which it "sounds the depths of [its] true being." This is the sphere of life before the Fall that comes closest to us through the deed of Christ:

Thus to the World-All speaks
In self-forgetfulness
And mindful of its primal state,
The growing human I:
In you, if I can free myself

From fetters of my selfhood,
I fathom my essential being.

In verse 4 cosmic light makes its first appearance in a way that celebrates what perceptive feeling (also translated as *sentience*) can and wants to contribute in future to the power of thinking. Verse 5 brings back with force the theme of cosmic life:

Within the light that out of spirit depths
Weaves germinating power into space
And manifests the gods' creative work:
Within its shine, the soul's true being
Is widened into worldwide life
And resurrected
From narrow selfhood's inner power.

It is this expansion into worldwide life of our cosmic origin that allows the human being to overcome herself, though as verse 2 has already indicated, something will have to rise from within to make this possible. Once we start resurrecting from "narrow selfhood's inner power" boding/intuition can "take up with strength [its] rightful task" as we are told in verse 7, which completes the quadrant.

Memory

Memory plays a cardinal role in the Spring Equinox quadrant. It is evoked at the turning point of the warning verse that inaugurates the period. In verse 46 we read:

The world is threatening to stun
The inborn forces of my soul;
Now, memory, come forth
From spirit depths, enkindling light;
Invigorate my inward sight
Which only by the strength of will
Is able to sustain itself.

101

It is interesting to notice that to a threat coming from the external world, the soul calls forth inner light and inward sight and an exertion of the will. To the world's call of the senses threatening to split asunder the forces of the soul, the response needs to come from spirit depths and through will exertion. In the fall, a self-engendered will allows us to turn vigorously to the needs of the world. In the spring an equivalent effort of the will is called forth, but this is turned inward with the aim of preparing the soul to be a receptacle of the forces coming from the cosmos, at a time in which the human being enters a period of nature consciousness.

The call to the power of memory is then followed by the culmination of the power of thinking in verses 47 to 49. In verse 47 the joy of growth has to find its match with the strength of thought. In 48 it is no longer just a strong thought, but a culminating certainty of cosmic thinking that renders the human being truly free, and thus able to pour transformative love into his deeds. The force of thought in the human being meets with the transformed thinking in verses 48 to 50.

In verse 49, already mentioned above, thinking's clarity intuits its kinship with the force of cosmic life. It does so by "recalling its own spirit growth through nights of cosmic darkness." Here memory brings, so to speak, the winter time to a close. Thinking crowns the winter's night with hope and recognizes the coming cosmic day. By looking back to the growth of the soul in which it had a major part, thinking knows it is prepared to meet the forces of cosmic life. And in the next verse the reverse happens. It is the joy of growth/cosmic life that recognizes the fulness of its being and meaning in the human being. The spirit world seeks itself and its completion in human existence.

Verses 51 to 1 express outwardly the glory of the senses' revelation, inwardly the permeation of the human being by the realm of cosmic life. This is expressed in many ways: cosmic spirit (51); life of worlds, strength of life, spirit's being (52); sun, spirit's life (1). Verse 2 echoes the theme of 50 that indicates the desire of the spirit worlds to seek themselves in the human being. Already in verse 51 it is indicated that we cannot just be content with sense impressions. We need to find what speaks in them through the spirit. And in verse 2, even though we grow in the sphere of cosmic life for the rejoicing of spirit worlds, we are reminded that we need to find the fruit of soul within ourselves.

Verse 3 indicates what this seeking within ourselves may mean:

Thus to the World-All speaks,
In self-forgetfulness
And mindful of its primal state,
The growing human I . . .

In memory, awakened in the sphere of cosmic life by Christ, we reconnect to that state of paradisial union in which humanity finds/remembers its true being. It is as if Christ brought us back to a knowledge of our essential nature, from which we have divorced ourselves ("mindful of its primal state"). We are in a state of memory, which is identification; this is why it can also be "self-forgetfulness." In the primal Edenic state we were not self-aware. Memory has become in the fullest sense Spirit Recollection. It is a memory of the evolution of the human, not just individual memory, but a reconnection to primordial humanity.

Now the ego senses that it needs to give itself up to what comes from the cosmos, no matter what it has acquired from the fall/winter time through hard work. The ego/self of the present is nothing in comparison to the Spirit Self that can in future be. We must consciously sacrifice the lower to let the higher grow in us. More can be said about the place of memory in the course of the year. We will return to it in the next chapter.

Voices in the Spring Verses

We have seen the voices that speak in alternation in the Summer Solstice quadrant. Something of the same nature occurs in the lead up to it in the preceding quadrant.

Verses 46 to 52
Verse 46 is the first to announce the risk offered by the call of the senses: "the world is threatening to stun the inborn forces of my soul." And it makes appeal to memory and the need to invigorate the inward sight that has been awakened through the spirit-birth.

In verse 49, shown above, clarity of thought speaks "I feel the force of cosmic life." Thinking recognizes the same force that manifests outwardly in the formative forces and inwardly as thought. Not surprisingly a response to this is offered by the force of cosmic life itself in verse 50. The joy of growth speaks: "I carry into you my life from its enchanted bondage and so attain my true goal."

Creation finds itself fulfilled in the human being, which is what the threshold verse 33 announced: the desire of world's reality to re-create itself in the souls which will strive for self-cognition and spiritualized thinking.

Verses 1 to 6

In verse 1 "the sun speaks to the human mind," but there is no content of a speech as such. In verse 3 the human I "to the World-All speaks" in a state of reminiscence of its primal state: this is the first, faint, announcement of the future role of intuition. The first verses indicate that Easter has brought a big change for the souls who actively seek the Christ. Through the Christ they feel the presence of the paradisal envelope of cosmic life, and of the world where the soul truly belongs from the time preceding the Fall.

In verse 4 perceptive feeling speaks and wants to add its influence to thinking's clarity, and unite the world and the human being, a theme that has been present since Easter. Verse 4 confirms that the soul can belong to the world in a more intimate way through Christ. And perceptive feeling, a close ally of intuition, shows us what summer will contribute to thinking, adding warmth to it.

The voices we hear in the Calendar at this time of the year alternate between microcosm (thinking) to macrocosm (joy of growth, sun) and back to the microcosm (human I and perceptive feeling). Notice also that there is a certain symmetry in the speaking: voices appear in verses 3 and 50 of cross 3 and 4 and 49 of cross 4.

Thinking speaks before the sphere of cosmic life responds and announces the change that is about to come. The human I responds by showing a new, though dim, awareness of itself as something larger that lives in the World-All. When we see that perceptive feeling speaks in the next verse and how it wants to complement thinking, we realize that the spring has been preparing the shift from thinking to intuition, whose role will be consecrated in the threshold verse 7.

The time of Easter is a time of transition. The more active presence of the Christ and the re-enlivening of nature and of our soul can only be achieved in a state of balance between the adversaries. On one hand we can carry on from the winter our desire to resort to an unmodified thinking. On the other we can lose ourselves all too readily in the world of germinating growth and in the appeal of the senses. Christ affects the balance between the forces of our soul and shows us the way to health. Balance comes from letting go of what comes from the winter and in taking in the strong impulse of the cosmic life that could throw us off balance. Our strengthened sense of Self is faced with the sobering reality that there is much still that we have to change in ourselves, and that we have to start as if anew and surrender not to the senses but to cosmic life, cosmic light, and cosmic warmth to be reborn in Christ.

II. Fall and Michaelmas

The Michaelmas Imagination

In summer the organism is permeated by the sulphur process, corresponding to combustion processes. For this reason, seen from the cosmos the inner being of the human being begins to shine. Ahriman, however, wants to draw the human being into a state of half-conscious sleep and dream. This is countered in the summer with the meteor showers and their cosmic iron, a healing force that the gods bring to bear against Ahriman through Micha-el.

The counterpart of this is the action of iron in the human blood, which undergoes a change toward fall. The human blood "is rayed through with the force which is carried as iron into the blood and wages war there on anxiety, fear and hate." It is as if in the blood "my life is full of shooting-stars, miniature shooting-stars."[40] At the same time the sulphur process radiates from the nerve system to the brain in opposition to the action of the iron process in the blood, which radiates from the head toward the bloodstream.

In the fall we are starting to experience the waning of nature in our

---

[40] Rudolf Steiner, *Four Seasons and the Archangels*, lecture 1.

inner self, and we must transition from nature consciousness, which would lead us downward, to self-consciousness. The human being can awaken from the experience of summer and acquire deeper consciousness of what this meant. The above is revealed by the form of Micha-el opposing the dragon. Michaelmas must become a festival for conquering fear and anxiety. On one hand we have to overcome love of ease and on the other unfold courageous activity and initiative, supported by a strong will.

The imagination of Micha-el arises from the cosmos; the dragon forms his body out of the arising sulphur streams. The space over which Micha-el rises in opposition to the dragon is filled with showers of meteoric iron. "These showers take form from the power that streams out from Michael's heart; they are welded together into the sword of Michael."[41]

The human being must turn his attention in our time from the prevailing industrial use of iron, which turns us toward materialism, to the meteoric iron which reminds us of the power of the spirit, which Micha-el forges; we must turn from natural science to spiritual science.

Some of the themes that we encounter in the fall are those of sleeping and waking, awakening of the will and summer of the soul (Figure 13).

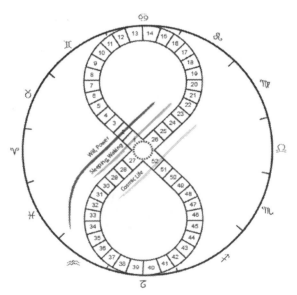

Figure 13: Themes in the Fall Equinox Quadrant

---

[41] Rudolf Steiner, *Four Seasons and the Archangels*, lecture 1.

Sleeping and Waking

We will look at the period leading to Michaelmas (verses 21 to 26) and the following one leading to the threshold verse (33).

Verses 21 to 26
The theme of sleeping and waking is completely framed within the Fall Equinox quadrant; it goes from verses 23 to 30. The interval is preceded by the awakening to the self: "selfhood power" in 21; "self of man" in 22, and immediately after by "soul life becomes aware of Self" in 24. The first mention of sleeping/waking is in verse is in verse 23:

> There dims in damp autumnal air
> The senses' luring magic;
> The light's revealing radiance
> Is dulled by hazy veils of mist.
> In distances around me I can see
> The autumn's winter sleep;
> The summer's life has yielded
> Itself into my keeping.

When all of nature retreats from the senses' revelation, the soul is tempted to follow the natural movement toward sleep. Micha-el asks us to counter this movement in the following verses. After "soul life becomes aware of Self" (verse 24) the theme of awakening enters in verse 25:

> I can belong now to myself
> And shining spread my inner light
> Into the dark of space and time.
> Toward sleep is urging all creation,
> But inmost soul must stay awake
> And carry wakefully sun's glowing
> Into the winter's icy flowing.

This gesture announces the Michaelic soul mood following immediately in the Michael verse (26), one of energetic call to action. The theme of awakening is more explicitly restated in verse 27:

When to my being's depths I penetrate,
There stirs expectant longing [prophetic intuition]
That self-observing, I may find myself
As gift of summer sun, a seed
That warming lives in autumn mood
As germinating force of soul.

The verses are immediately followed by the continuation of the awakening to the Self (verses 26, 27) and the rising of the role of thinking in the soul (28 to 30). When "flourish in the sunlight of my soul the ripened fruits of thinking" the I is able to "perceive now joyfully the autumn's spirit-waking" in verse 30:

There flourish in the sunlight of my soul
The ripened fruits of thinking;
To conscious self-assurance
The flow of feeling is transformed.
I can perceive now joyfully
The autumn's spirit-waking:
The winter will arouse in me
The summer of the soul.

The "autumn's winter sleep" (verse 23) has now been overcome in the soul, which can now joyfully perceive the "autumn's spirit-waking." This movement has been supported first by the soul's awareness of the self, then by the growing power of thought.

Will, Strength, Power

Verses 21 to 26
The first appearance of the theme is preceded with the mention of "strange power . . . gaining strength" and "selfhood's power" in 21, one of the first verses to speak of the emerging self (verses 16, 21, 22). In verse 24 we hear of the Michaelic "self-engendered will," fruit of the effort of self-cognition:

Unceasingly itself creating,
Soul life becomes aware of self;
The cosmic spirit, striving on,
Renews itself by self-cognition,
And from the darkness of the soul
Creates the fruit of self-engendered will.

Verse 25 enjoins us to remain awake while all arounds us nature moves to sleep. Verse 26 of Micha-el is all will:

O Nature, your maternal life
I bear within the essence of my will.
And my will's fiery energy
Shall steel my spirit striving,
That sense of self springs froth from it
To hold me in myself.

The rallying cry of Michael's sword and his meteoric iron present themselves to our imagination in his call to steel our spirit striving.

Verses 27 to 33
We enter the verses of emergence of the force of thought, and here will appears in the mention of the "cosmic spirit fount of strength" that allows us to "read life's inner meaning." (29)

To fan the spark of thinking into flame
By my own strong endeavor,
To read life's inner meaning
Out of the cosmic spirit's fount of strength:
This is my summer heritage,
My autumn solace, and my winter hope.

This is a call to energetic exertion of our will forces through the faculty of thinking and through our determined presence in the world. Wisdom marries strength. Verse 32 is another culmination; it reads

I feel my own force, bearing fruit
And gaining strength to give me to the world.
My inmost being I feel charged with power
To turn with clearer insight
Toward the weaving of life's destiny.

This verse gives us the feeling of the soul at home in the world and confident in its ability to meet its challenges. In verse 34, just after the threshold verse, it is the new risen sense of Self that gives us the possibility to pour cosmic forces into our deeds:

In secret inwardly to feel
How all that I've preserved of old
Is quickened by new-risen sense of self:
This shall, awakening, pour forth cosmic forces
Into the outer actions of my life
And growing, mould me into true existence.

The undifferentiated self-engendered will, which has just emerged from the darkness of the soul (verse 24), becomes the ability to be present in the world with strength and insight and to pour cosmic forces into our deeds. Notice also the transition point of Michaelmas. Before this the will emerges that culminates in the forging of the Michaelic sword. After this much of the will goes into the forging of the power of thinking.

Summer of the Soul

All of spring and summer relate to the power of the sun, to cosmic light and cosmic warmth in one form or another. It is the sun who speaks to the human mind in the very first verse, the one of Easter. The sun is present in the following spring verses through its light and warmth.

We pass through 20 into the third mid-season quadrant with a significant shift. The sun becomes the spent summer given to the human being in 23.

Verses 21 to 26

When everything around in nature fades, something remains as a fruit in the soul. In a verse of maximum contraction (23) a seed remains planted in the soul.

> There dims in damp autumnal air
> The senses' luring magic;
> The light's revealing radiance
> Is dulled by hazy veils of mist.
> In distances around me I can see
> The autumn's winter sleep;
> The summer's life has yielded
> Itself into my keeping.

Two new faculties appear in 25: inner light and wakefulness of soul. The human being carries light into the dark through the inner sun's glowing, another expression of summer of the soul, and this is followed by the strong stirring into inner activity of the Michaelmas verse.

Verses 27 to 33

In 27 the Self is called "a gift of summer sun, a seed" that germinates:

> . . . As gift of summer sun, a seed
> That warming lives in autumn mood
> As germinating force of soul.

The activities that take place outwardly in the spring are now landscapes of the soul; we have seeds, warmth, and germination, but as pure presences in the soul. Now thinking rises to its full power when we hear about "the radiance of my thought coming from soul's Sun power" in verse 28:

> I can, in newly quickened inner life,
> Sense wide horizons in myself.
> The force and radiance of my thought—
> Coming from soul's sun power—
> Can solve the mysteries of life,

And grant fulfilment now to wishes
Whose wings have long been lamed by hope.

The sun of the soul's landscape is now clearly associated to the power of thinking, which can carry the light and warmth through the winter. And the capacity of activating thinking and the will are called summer heritage in verse 29. In verse 30 the summer of the soul is mentioned for the last time, and here thinking and feeling support each other and affirm the self:

There flourish within the sunlight of my soul
The ripened fruits of thinking;
To conscious self-assurance
The flow of feeling is transformed.
I can perceive now joyfully
The autumn's spirit-waking:
The winter will arouse in me
The summer of the soul.

What was just a spent summer in verse 23 has become through the vigorous effort requested by Micha-el an autumn's spirit waking and an affirmative summer of the soul. In essence we have the inner sun of intuition in the spring to summer time of the year, which allows us not to get lost in the floods of light and warmth and in the intoxicating dream. In the fall and winter the inner light and power of thinking allow us to remain awake and direct our will outwardly when we would tend to retreat inwardly.

In the summer Ahriman attempts to induce the human being into a state of semi-consciousness and sleep. In the fall Micha-el rises against him and calls the human being to emerge from the nature consciousness of the summer and to develop consciousness of self. The sulphur process activates the power of thought; the meteoric iron strengthens the will and allows us to overcome fear and anxiety.

The human being can internalize and raise to fuller understanding the experience of the summer and bring to maturity a summer of the soul. It is through energetic stirring and striving that the inner sword of Michael is forged, particularly through our thinking, which becomes the light that shines in the darkness of the elements. To do this we have to overcome love of ease and develop the courage needed to confront the dragon.

What was cosmic life in the spring verses has now become the Michaelic will in the fall. Whereas in the winter to spring verses the last embers of thinking lead us to Easter (verses 48 and 1) and intuition emerges at the end of the cycle, here the contrary happens; intuition supports the movement toward greater awareness of self (verses 21 and 27), then passes on the baton immediately after to thinking. The external sun becomes the summer of the soul that will guide us through the winter.

CHAPTER 7

~~~Ꮼ~~~

THE MID-SEASON
QUADRANTS IN REVIEW

This chapter will gather the insights formed so far. Before reviewing the whole we will explore another contrast: that of the expression of the will in the two halves of the year.

Dream, Sleep, Memory, and Self-Engendered Will

Enlivened Remembrance

In the spring and summer part of the year the soul tends to excarnate under the pull of the senses. This is what the Calendar warns us about first in the threshold verses 46 and 7. In the first we are told that "the world is threatening to stun the inborn forces of my soul"; in the second that "My Self is threatening to fly forth lured strongly by the world's enticing light." What we must do is clearly specified in verse 7 itself: "Come forth, prophethic feeling [boding], take up with strength your rightful task: replace in me the power of thought which in the senses' glory would gladly lose itself." What threatens the human being is what we could call the "dream." In verse 8 we are told that "the senses' might . . . presses down my power of thinking into a dreamlike dullness" and that "must human thinking in quiet dream-life rest content."

The danger of sinking into a dream consciousness is brought forth again in verses 8, 14, and 15. It culminates in verse 15, just after the beginning of the summer descending phase, in enchanted weaving enveloping the human being in order to let the divine "bestow the strength which in its narrow bounds my I is powerless to give itself." This last sentence indicates clearly what is the purpose of "dreaming" and surrendering: to let the spirit world lend us strength. We awaken immediately from the dream when we are asked to "bear in inward keeping spirit bounty" in verse 16. In verse 19 this effort goes a step further in the will with the intention to "encompass now with memory what I've newly got."

Even before the specific verse 19, the act of remembering is pointed at indirectly. In verse 17 the soul recognizes that godly power announced in verse 10 as the cosmic Word. Guided by this recognition and memory, however dim, verse 18 echoes the stern command of verse 16 "of bearing in inward keeping spirit bounty" by strengthening the striving to take responsibility for our lives and strengthening ourselves in view of the end of summer.

The awakening from the dream requires an effort of the will, and that takes the form of memory. This is the equivalent of the effort we need to apply in the morning when we want to remember a significant dream. Here we are trying to recapture a midsummer night's dream, so to speak. And 19 comes just before the "warning" verse 20 in which we are asked to feel our life's reality in conjunction with the world's existence: to fully awaken to ourselves.

The danger lies in the light and warmth of cosmic light and cosmic warmth retreating and the soul not being able to strengthen awareness of Self. Memory plays an important role in the strengthening of the Self. Therefore a look at the power of memory shall highlight its key role.

In rising from the forming of mental images to that of memories, we have to push our inner activity into a deeper part of our being, into the etheric body. The store of images remains in the etheric body and is not allowed to rise into the physical body. This means that something lives in our body that does not and cannot influence the physical body. This is like a seed that does not unfold its powers in this life.

When the spiritual world starts to open up for us, or when we come to the gate of death, the soul lives first in that part which has not touched the physical body. In Steiner's words, "The power of memory may be said to be the very beginning of a spiritual element in us. . . . the store of memories in the inner life marks the first stage of transition from things that are bound to the senses and the brain, to something that is pure inner life and spirit."[42] The memories become objective reality around us, and looking at them the spiritual investigator perceives powers of a still higher kind from which arise Imaginations. These are the same powers of the soul that bring about the dissolution of the images a few days after death. Herein lies the importance of exerting our faculty of memory at the end of summer, just like we do at the end of our lives on earth.

Self-Engendered Will

Where do we find the counterpart to the condition of dream in the fall-winter part of the year? We see it before and after Michaelmas, roughly between verses 23 and 30. The interval is preceded by the awakening to the self: "selfhood's power" in 21; "the human self" in 22, and immediately after by the important turning point of the "soul life becomes aware of Self" (24).

The first mention of the theme of sleeping/waking is found in verse 23: "in distances around me I can see the autumn's winter sleep" (23). After "soul life becomes aware of Self" (24) the theme of awakening enters in: "toward sleep is urging all creation, but inmost soul must stay awake and carry wakefully sun's glowing into the winter's icy flowing" (25). The verses are immediately followed by the awakening to the Self (26, 27) and the rising of the role of thinking in the soul (28 to 30). When "flourish in the sunlight of my soul ripened fruits of thinking" the I is able to "perceive now joyfully the autumn's spirit-waking" (30). The external state of sleep is countered by the soul's ability to stay fully awake in thinking.

In the summer the soul risks entering a state of dream and losing self-connection. In the fall another threat engulfs the soul: not that of dream, but of sleep. Awakening of the self and rising of the faculty of thinking go hand in hand. It is through these that the cold time of the year can present the opportunity to awaken to self and clear cognition, to cast light into the darkness through our thinking; to be awake at the time of outer sleep, to project outward our inner warmth at the time of greatest cold. Something similar to verse 19 appears in verse 46, which is almost its opposite. But here something more is at play, because 46 is also a threshold verse, which sets the tone for the whole of the Spring Equinox quadrant.

---

[42] Rudolf Steiner: *The Inner Nature of Man*, lectures of April 8, 1914.

In winter we can ultimately reach the stage of co-creators and contribute consciously to the world of creation. At the end of the Winter Solstice quadrant (verse 46) memory is called forth to gather, not all the fruits bestowed by the spirit world, but those produced by the human being. We do not just "encompass now with memory" (verse 19) but call forth memory and strength of will. Let us see how the stage is set.

Verses 43 to 45 form a crescendo of the light of thinking and warmth of heart: "inner fire" (43); "soul clarity," "spirit-birth," and "creative will of my own thinking" (44); "light of thinking" (45). What we are facing is not due to lack of inner preparation; rather, it is the onslaught of a new presence and force. It is what shines behind the life and tone ethers: cosmic life that will enter in full swing at the time of Easter.

After the warning verse, thinking is called to reach yet another stage: strength of thought well-armed by powers divine (47); certainty of cosmic thinking that "awakens love" (48); clarity of thought (49). These develop in parallel with the growing power of cosmic life that was not mentioned before 46: joy of growth (47, 50); force of cosmic life (49).

We must let go of too formed a sense of self when cosmic life challenges us to live in depths of soul. When we remember again our efforts through the winter, in 49 it is clear that these can be attributed to our clarity of thought "recalling its own spirit growth through nights of cosmic darkness." In verse 49, which reminds us of the importance of verse 46, memory allows us to hold this perspective. Memory, looking backward, offers us confidence in what is to come. The content of memory relates to the past; the exertion of memory opens doors for the future, and this is visible in the following verses.

The faculty of memory is a power of "inner sight" as specified in verse 46, which once cultivated, allows us to reach seership. After the passing of winter, the soul can loosen its identification with what it has conquered of the Self, while memory calls forth other powers when the faculties of the soul risk separating from each other under the pull of the senses. Through the strengthening of memory the experience of the winter will remain as a seed to guide us through the spring and summer, when the power of thinking will gradually ebb.

We strengthen the power of memory through the daily practice of the *rückschau*. As another example, this power of memory can also be cultivated as a conscious exercise in relation to a deceased loved one by recalling common experiences, and eventually it can lead us to an encounter with her in the spirit.

The Disciples cultivated the power of memory after the Resurrection in order to enliven their store of experiences with Christ and to find Him again in the sphere of the etheric. They brought back to enlivened memory His words and deeds. This force of recollection brought Him back among them, as in the Emmaus experience. From memory arose revelation; His words and deeds acquired new meaning. And these events occurred just after the time of the year of which we are talking here, after the changes brought about by the historical Resurrection.

The enhanced faculty of recollection will allow us to develop organs of perception for the spiritual, which will strengthen the voice of conscience and give us guidance for the present and the future. Through this enhanced remembrance we call our angel and other spiritual beings to our help. Here lies its importance at the end of the Winter Solstice quadrant.

Memory continues to play an important part both in looking backward to the winter part of the year and in exerting itself to prepare the transition to spring. The first role, as we saw, appears in verse 49. After thinking sings its swan song in verses 1 and 2 ("the power of thought gives up its separate being") memory plays a role preparing to the challenges of the spring in verse 3, just as verse 46 announced.

Thus to the World-All speaks,
In self-forgetfulness
And mindful of its primal state,
The growing human I:
In you, if I can free myself
From fetters of my selfhood,
I fathom my essential being.

The power of memory once again plays a paradoxical role between past and future. Keeping in mind that the spirit world discovers and seeks itself in the human being (verse 2), the human being answers in verse 3 by "finding the fruit of soul within itself." This finding occurs through an awakening of enlivened memory of the human being's primal state, in effect a distant memory of the primal condition of humanity, that of original participation in which it lived in the World-All; the memory of the time before the Fall. Memory brought to its ultimate power transcends the boundaries of life between birth and death; it is memory of the original human being. It is this memory that is the key to transcending the narrow bounds of self (fetters of selfhood), a recurring theme of the spring. In light of the memory of who we are meant to be and can become anew, we can act out of self-forgetfulness renounce the limits of who we are at present, no matter how hard wrought the achievements reached through the winter trials.

The effort of memory goes on from verse 46 at the end of winter to verse 19 at the end of the midsummer quadrant. It serves as a reminder of the work that the soul has accomplished and of the inner fruits it has gathered through the midwinter. Then memory becomes universal human memory of the archetypal human condition, of its primeval union in the bosom of the Gods. Verse 3 exemplifies this state of soul. Once past verse 7 memory serves a different role; it brings to light those experiences that the soul has lived in a dreamy state. Verse 8 indicates that "human thinking [must] in quiet dream-life rest content." In verse 10 I am offered the indication that I "shall in future know: a godly being now has touched [me]." Verse 14 reminds us that we have lived through the summer as if we had "lost the drive of [our] own being and dreamlike thinking seemed to daze and rob [us] of [our Self]." In verse 15 our own Self has been enwrapped in "enchanted weaving of spirit within outer glory." It is all these experiences, lived beyond the threshold of consciousness, that we are asked to evoke and raise to consciousness in verse 19, so that we can better cultivate the "fruits of selfhood" (16) and selfhood's forces (19).

Self-Engendered Will
The act of remembering and perceiving memory pictures by the ego works from the physical body through the forming of mental images into the soul. The ego brings about a polar gesture in the act of will, in which the soul carries will impulses into the world through the physical body. In the act of will, the ego acts out of the warmth ether and through this unites

with the warmth organism. As a result the combustion processes in the metabolism are enhanced.[43]

The will appears in many ways in the period going from threshold verses 20 to 46 and shortly after in close association with the emergence of the conscious Self after the dream of summer. Let us see how.

In verse 24 "soul life becomes aware of Self" and "self-engendered will" emerges from the "darkness of the soul." Now it wants to exert itself in the world. The Michaelmas verse, all strength of will, is worth being quoted in full once more. Here its link to cosmic life, in the form of Nature's maternal life, is made explicit.

> O Nature, your maternal life
> I bear within the essence of my will.
> And my will's fiery energy
> Shall steel my spirit striving,
> That sense of self springs forth from it
> To hold me in myself.

The power of will gradually appears transformed into will-permeated thinking, starting from verse 28. Here the power of thought "can solve the mysteries of life, and grant fulfilment now to wishes . . . long lamed by hope." The desire to imbue thinking with self-engendered will is further encapsulated in verse 29's "fan the spark of thinking into flame."

The will emerges in pure fashion in verse 31 where mention is given of "forceful will of life" that ultimately create the conditions for "human deeds." This desire to be of service to the world is echoed in 32 where the strength we feel in ourselves is there to "give me to the world" and "turn with clearer insight toward the weaving of life's destiny." Soon after the themes woven so far enhance each other in the desire, not only to serve the world, but to "pour forth cosmic forces into the outer actions of my life" (34). Verses 36 through 40 no doubt bring our self-engendered will through a deep maturation through the conscious receiving of the cosmic Word, the maturation of the spirit-birth, and the influence of the Spirit Self.

When willing wants to express itself anew in the world, it is colored

---

[43] Rudolf Steiner, *Eight Lectures to Doctors*, lecture of January 2nd 1924.

by powers of the heart and the soul's yearning for love. In verse 41 the soul wants to "kindle and enflame God-given powers in human life to right activity" and "[shape] itself in human loving and in human working." In the following verses the soul, animated by forces of the heart and imbued with growing love, can withstand cold and darkness to assist in the work of creation, in becoming co-creator. This is the ultimate blossoming of self-engendered will.

As the sphere of cosmic life grows closer in coming to Spring and Easter, the power of thought acquires new brilliance and becomes cosmic thinking, the ultimate will-imbued thinking that connects us directly to cosmic thoughts at work in the macrocosm. This is particularly visible in verses 44, 45, 47, and 48. In the last verse it is cosmic thinking that allows to "awaken love" no longer just in myself, but "in human hearts." What was previously "human loving" (verse 41) is now objective, cosmic love.

As the realm of cosmic life expresses itself anew in "joy of growth," the will expresses itself in a purer way as desire to "renew its strength" (51), bring "life-strength into human bodies" (52), or in "spirit worlds . . . [germinate]" (2).

Let us recapture the journey of self-engendered will. We see it first expressed as the desire to awaken the self and express itself in deeds. This mingles with the effort to metamorphose and spiritualize human thinking. In conjunction with the work of cosmic Word and the Self being touched by the Spirit Self, the soul awakens in the heart and so does the will. The light of will-imbued thinking is deepened and transformed into the power of love. As cosmic life approaches in the wake of the Christ's being at Easter, thinking recedes not without offering its last fruits and strengthening the human being to receive the impulse of growth in nature. Self-engendered will, strengthened and purified, can now receive the Christ impulse in a state of genuine soul innocence.

Mental Images and Actions

Judgments that we make lie at the beginning of and evolve into mental images. A mental image of the concept "tree" embodies a great number of smaller images (living and growing being, trunk, crown of foliage, upward striving nature, etc.). The overall mental image and the mental images that build it are all derived from judgments. When the human being evolves and acquires a discerning and precise thinking, "the judgment corresponds to the mental image and thereby gains clearer outlines. As an image it is projected to the border between soul and world [and placed in front of the I]."[44] Judging itself takes place in the soul. In the forming of an image, something dynamic in the world comes to rest in the soul; an event or being becomes an image. As to the activity of the forming of mental images, Zeylmans van Emmichoven has this to say: "Forming of mental images is indeed a condensation into images, but it occurs when the soul directs itself to the spirit."[45]

The higher the maturity we reach, the higher the array of mental images that lives in our soul. And the more the individual strives toward self-development, the more the images will evolve. In mental images there is an element of feeling; we form varying degrees of attachment to the images. And they are also associated with an element of desire; the images cause a deeper or shallower degree of satisfaction. The more we exert ourselves intellectually and spiritually, the more satiated will we be. The soul needs mental images like the body needs nourishment. It wants to acquire new mental images or improve existing ones.

Among and above all images there is a central one that arises from the core of the soul without any connection with anything else: the image of the "I." All other images in the soul are closely connected to this image.

The activity of the soul in summer, in the fullness of nature-consciousness, does in effect lead to the awakening of the powers of selfhood, and the activity of remembering at the end of summer anchors it (see verses 20 and 21). The whole movement is perfected and brought into full consciousness during the fall and winter, the time of self-consciousness, through the desire of the soul to act in the world through sacrifice. During the summer pole of the calendar, the will is as if directed inwardly through intuition; during the winter pole, it works itself outwardly through thinking. Devotion to the spirit and acceptance of inner powerlessness in summer becomes sacrifice and love in the winter time of the year.

---

[44] F. W. Zeylmans van Emmichoven, *The Anthroposophical Understanding of the Human Soul*, 43.

[45] F. W. Zeylmans van Emmichoven, *The Anthroposophical Understanding of the Human Soul*, 44.

Powerlessness and Sacrifice

In the summer pole of the year memory works hand in hand with intuition. The letting go of the first quarter of the year (verses 1 to 13) means reaching a place of powerlessness, or rather apparent powerlessness. In utter trust we give ourselves to cosmic light and cosmic warmth, to the realm of the First Hierarchy and to the cosmic Word. New directions will emerge of which the human being knows nothing in his daily consciousness; he can only intuit. We literally trust that something better than what our consciousness can fathom will meet us if we follow the dictates of our conscience through intuition. In this context memory is something more than what we apprehend normally; it becomes enlivened remembrance. Perceived powerlessness leads us to the receiving of cosmic thinking, the cosmic intelligence of the hierarchies working in unison. It becomes the avenue for letting go and letting come, for a new way of being in the world. The second part of the summer (verses 14 to 26) crystallizes the new evolutionary possibilities; it gives them direction and strength.

At the other end of the year, the preparation lies in consciously letting our sense of self unfold and grow, in developing the Michaelic, and universal, self-engendered will that prepares us to receive the cosmic Word more consciously. What the human being has wrested from the spiritual world generates an overabundance from which the tempered will can now transform the self in thinking, feeling, and willing. Just as in summer the cosmic world pours into us its overabundance of forces, the earth now contracted into itself is waiting for the human being to give of his newly generated inner substance. The earth is calling for the human being to be a co-creator, and the conscious human being will naturally find the strength to sacrifice its personal goals at the altar of world evolution.

We can revisit the earlier example drawn from Steiner's life under this light. It was an epochal decision to accept Karl Julius Schröer's task as his own, and this did not happen overnight. Steiner had already found his natural karmic companions within the circles of the Cistercians.[46] He expressed how a deep love united him to them. He accepted the utter powerlessness of renouncing the natural links of destiny. This would lead

---

[46] See Luigi Morelli, *Karl Julius Schröer and Rudolf Steiner: Anthroposophy and the Teachings of Karma and Reincarnation*, Chapter 1: Karl Julius Schröer's and Rudolf Steiner's Missions.

him over time into the utterly karmically foreign milieu of Theosophy in order to develop his new task. He thus renounced for a long spell of time to bring to civilization the new Christianized teachings of karma and reincarnation. Indeed he had no idea of how and when these would be possible for him again.

To the inwardly active task of letting go and powerlessness corresponded the flip side of the coin of actively taking on something new, of taking on the new task of bringing to the world the legacy of the scientific Goethe that would lead to spiritual science. This was his consciously performed act of sacrifice. Years of his life were devoted to doing what destiny had delegated to the reincarnated Plato.

In a similar fashion we can point to the experience of the Disciples after Easter. In the state of despair and inner powerlessness after the death of their teacher, new soul forces matured through the power of enlightened remembrance. It was in this way that the Christ appeared to many of them in his resurrected body. The experience of Pentecost was the Disciples' experience of resurrection. Later on they were able to take on their mission with a new conviction and zeal. They naturally sacrificed themselves to hostile forces in order serve the new communities and spread the Christ impulse.

When we review the year according to the expressions of the self and the engagement of the will, we can do so returning to the season's quadrants (1 to 13, 14 to 26, 27 to 39, 40 to 52). The turning points become the solstices and equinoxes. During the spring time of the year the soul actively lets go of the attachments of the lower self; we could call this a time of letting go of narrow boundaries of self. It is a time of catharsis and purification. Around the time of St. John the soul has reached what feels like powerlessness from the perspective of the ego; in reality it is an openness to a higher and truer power, to the influx of cosmic Word and cosmic thinking. The whole of summer is a time of allowing the spirit world to work in us, until selfhood power takes root in the soul. The Sun of the summer becomes a sun and summer of the soul from which emerges the sense of Self.

The gesture of spring and summer is mirrored in fall and winter. The fall is a time for strengthening resolve in our will, for imbuing our will selflessly for the good. Christmas is the time of spirit-birth, fruit of a raising to consciousness of the cosmic Word through the instrument of a will-imbued thinking. Cosmic Word takes residence in the soul, but this time more consciously than in the summer. After the spirit-birth, the strengthened resolves of the will become active capacity to sacrifice our personal aims to objective world needs, to joyfully understand, internalize, and embrace new aims. Through sacrifice we know love in our hearts and spread love in the world.

If in the spring and summer we experience the powerlessness of our daily ego and the need to enrich it from spiritual heights, then in winter to spring, the final sacrifice to accomplish is that of our identification with the fruits of selfhood we have wrested through the cold time of the year. It's not our higher self that we could ever possibly sacrifice; rather our identification with what we have achieved through personal effort. The soul knows that no matter how much it has gained, much work remains to be done. It is ready to start again, each year possibly at a higher level, and let Christ imbue it with fresh energies from cosmic realms at the time of Easter.

Quadrants and Soul Faculties

The threshold verses either directly and explicitly, or indirectly, point to the faculties that should arise at each of the times of the solstices and equinoxes. Explicitly, verse 46 calls for "now, memory, come forth." Memory allows the soul to undertake what amounts to the greatest transition in the calendar, the annual return to its starting point and animating point of origin, the cosmic/historic Christ impulse. On one hand it will remember and preserve its own acquired consciousness of self as long as possible, and on the other it will evoke its own original state of purity.

Verse 7 invokes "come forth intuition." This is the time of the summer and the peak of the ascent into what could be called "nature consciousness." The soul expands into the cosmos and intuition offers it a natural compass, allowing it to expand and lose itself to some extent in cosmic light and warmth, without losing the anchoring of the Self.

Verse 20 has no such explicit call. The nature of the call emerges through the quality of the verses and the time of Michaelmas. I call this the time of "come forth 'Self-engendered will'" (verse 24). In effect both the focus on the emerging Self and the stirring to vigorous, Michaelic action color the whole time of Michaelmas. The soul enters the time of self-consciousness. It awakens from the dream of summer and avoids the sleep of outer nature through vigorous inner activity.

To be sure, thinking emerges on the horizon soon after Michaelmas. It finds its confirmation through the cosmic Word at the Christmas spirit-birth. From achieved thinking radiates the human being's co-creative role in the macrocosmos and the force of love that colors the later part of the quadrant.

We can rename the four mid-season quadrants in keeping with their spirit. Verse 7 calls "come forth intuition." Likewise verse 20 could say "come forth, self-engendered will." Verse 33 would echo 7 in complementary fashion "come forth, clarity of thinking." Finally, 46 would contrast 20 with "come forth, enlivened remembrance."

Enlivened remembrance accompanies not just the Spring Equinox mid-season quadrant but also the Summer Solstice one, culminating in verse 19. Self-engendered will is polished and refined not just through the Michaelmas quadrant; it carries over into the Christmas and winter time of the year, culminating in the affirmation of human love (verse 48).

The Calendar of the Soul in Review

We will now retrace the course of the year in light of the themes that have emerged and in relation to the working of the beings of the First Hierarchy as they work through cosmic life, cosmic light, cosmic Word, and cosmic thinking.

Growing into Awakened Original Participation: Easter to Michaelmas

The verses of cross 7 form the boundaries and point to the task of each mid-season quadrant. The Spring Equinox quadrant tells us our task is to counter the tendency of the Self to "threaten to fly forth" (verse 7). It is achieved in 20 when "I feel at last my life's reality."

Verses 1 to 6: Spring Equinox Half Quadrant: Cosmic Life and Waning of the Sense of Self

The arrival of cosmic life is announced before Easter in verse 49. Life in all its forms (joy of growth, life of worlds [cosmic life], strength of life, spirit's life) irrupts more and more from the end of winter/early spring into the weeks that follow Easter. This is the realm that comes to us through the renewed presence of the Christ Mystery. If we look roughly at verses 1 to 6, we notice that the self is now perceived as something that has to be loosened and transformed. The human being who embraces the Christ impulse can only experience cosmic life indirectly through it. Cosmic light starts to add its effect in verses 4 and 5.

The soul faculty of remembrance forms the bridge from the winter to the spring. It carries the fruits of winter into the spring, reconnects us to our primeval self and to the inheritance of original participation in the workings of the cosmos.

Verses 7 to 20: Intuition and Renewing of Self

Verse 7 indicates that the movement initiated in the early spring can only continue if the human being does not lose himself in the enticing light. This is a difficult request; on one hand the soul must lose itself in light and warmth; on the other it cannot lose the presence of the ego. Intuition is that ability of walking the tightrope of loosening too tightly held a notion of personal identity without losing oneself in the attempt. This can only be done through a continuing fine listening to the dictates of the universe and the promptings of the soul. While we apparently excarnate and grow with the out-breathing of the universe into an unconscious participation—a nature consciousness—with our faculty of intuition we direct and navigate this delicate process of inner growth.

During the first part of the season (up to verse 13) we sacrifice our lower ego in order to expand our soul, cleanse it of its attachments, and entrust it to the cosmic light and cosmic warmth. At this juncture we come in contact with the realm of cosmic Word, not yet rendered conscious, bestowing His gifts upon us. Through intuition we can reach a state of apparent powerlessness, which is in reality our willingness to let cosmic Word work in us.

An important juncture is formed immediately after in verse 14, when we sense the approach of cosmic thinking. The end result of this is the working of the hierarchies in us, offering us intimations of what the future holds for us, upon which we can decide to embark in freedom. This we could say is the greatest gift of the height of summer.

During the second part of the summer and up to verse 19, we nurture and tend to the gifts received during the sun's ascending course. We are asked to seek expectantly, to bear in inward keeping, to imbue our spirit depths with cosmic Word's wide world-horizons, to expand our soul and fashion it worthily. This intense inner activity leads at the culmination of the process to an effort of recollection ("encompass now with memory") such that the soul knows that strengthening selfhood forces will be awakened from it. The end of the Summer Solstice quadrant leaves us with this promise.

Growing into Conscious Participation: Michaelmas to Easter

Verses 21 to 33: Fall Equinox Quadrant: Awakening to Self and to the Power of Thinking

The purpose of this time of the year is highlighted between verses 20 and 33. After sensing the reality of one's destiny ("I feel at last my life's reality") the soul is challenged to look outward at "the world's existence" in order to bring to birth the sense of Self that will first emerge in verse 26 and then come to birth at Christmas (verse 38). It is ushered in by verse 33 where the soul can "feel at last the world's reality."

After verse 20 reminds us of our responsibility toward world's existence, the soul knows it needs to impress a different direction to its efforts, chiefly a strengthening of the Self. We read expressions such as selfhood's power, awareness of Self, and sense of Self, especially in the verses leading to Michaelmas. The Michaelmas verse is a celebration of the self-engendered and Michaelic will. It also reveals that the sphere of cosmic life has been internalized (nature's "maternal life I bear within the essence of my will" in verse 26 of Michaelmas) and transformed into will of life that keeps egotism at bay. Behind it we can recognize the eternal fount of strength of the Thrones, through which the human being can purify his will.

After Michaelmas, verse after verse celebrates the rise of the power of thinking in expressions like "radiance of my thought," "spark of thinking into flame," there flourish in the sunlight of my soul the ripened fruits of thinking," and "clearer insight." Do we not recognize in the power of thinking the emerging sphere of cosmic light that the human being can make its own—no longer just receive, but radiate into the world? Thinking is this inner light that strives toward the Lights of the Stars and the eternal fount of light of the Cherubim.

Verses 33 to 45: Winter Solstice Quadrant: Strengthening of the Self and Spirit-Birth

The soul's capacity for co-creation is now met with the challenge of forming a deep connection with the created world to the point of being able to re-create it in one's soul (verse 33). The human being is called to be a co-creator. However, the true center of attention is "the world's reality." The spirit world seeks itself in the human realm; it wants to connect with the human soul and re-create itself therein.

The Michaelic will takes on a new dimension; it expresses itself in deeds and desire to transform the world of nature and of our relations in the Winter Solstice quadrant. At the beginning of the quadrant the desire of the self to purify its being in the cosmic Self and meet "true existence" calls forth cosmic Word (verses 36 to 40). At Christmas the cosmic Word that the individual has allowed in through the gate of the senses in summer (verse 17) is now something that the soul welcomes in full self-awareness. This is what the calendar calls the spirit-birth of Christmas. The blessed presence confers to our deeds a deeper imprint. It calls immediately to a purification. The soul now longs to express the newborn fire of the heart and transform it into warmth of deeds and love. The cosmic warmth of the eternal fount of the Seraphim imbues us and is transformed into the love of which the soul is capable. This warmth gives to the force of thinking power to reach to the formative forces that will express themselves in the joy of growth. Thinking prepares itself to meet the impetus of the rising cosmic life (joy of growth) though it also knows that it will have to recede. In the meantime this means that the forces of the soul run the risk of separating from each other.

Verses 47 to 7: Spring Equinox Quadrant to Easter: Cosmic Life and Waning of the Sense of Self

The challenge of this time of the year lies between two dangers: the separation of the forces of the soul (verse 46) and the Self losing itself in the pull of the light of summer (verse 7). The power of memory offers an inner compass.

Thinking reaches to the font from which the human being has been separated after the Fall, knowing that in future it can become human/cosmic thinking (verse 48), averting thus the danger announced in verse 46. However, because the forces of life come in force and thinking has to recede, the soul has to prepare itself to develop new capacities. Through the human being's newly acquired capacities, the spirit world can now seek itself in the human being, and this becomes the revelation that reaches its climax at Easter. The deed of Golgotha reverberates each year to start the cycle anew.

The Calendar of the Soul and the Round of the Years

In ending we can look at the dynamic qualities of the four quadrants. In spring the soul focuses on dissolving the narrow boundaries of the ego by letting in the Christ-enlivened spheres of cosmic life and cosmic light work upon the soul. Nature consciousness works in a receptive soul of mood. In summer the soul lives in a gesture of allowing/letting come of the spirit within itself. It nurtures and gives birth to selfhood power within the spheres of cosmic light and cosmic warmth. Nature consciousness takes on here a more active quality.

In the fall the soul is called to an energetic stirring. Cosmic life within awakens the strength and power related to the recognition of the emerging Self. Nature consciousness gives way to self-consciousness. In the winter the soul generates cosmic light and cosmic warmth of enlivened thinking and conscious sacrifice, generating love and offered to the world in an act of co-creation.

The Calendar of the Soul becomes thus that rhythmic alternation between self and universe in which we dip into the fountainhead of cosmic life, cosmic light, and cosmic warmth, then reproduce it in ourselves and pour new forces into the world; we purify our lower self and/or strengthen our higher self; we dream, tend to fall asleep, awake, and remember. In practicing this soul breathing in rhythmic alternation year after year, the feelings evoked by the verses will become more and more real and illuminate the accompanying intellectual content. We will develop steadiness of soul as we face the temptations of the various times of the year. These may not grow less, but we may grow more secure and steadfast, and better equipped to contribute to the world's evolving.

APPENDIX 1

‚‚‚‚‚‚ꟷℳꟷ‚‚‚‚‚‚

THE SEQUENCE OF THE VERSES: THEMES AND TRANSITIONS

When entering the Calendar of the Soul as a novice, and even after a number of years, the varieties of themes and their interlacing hid the perception of continuity for much of the parts of the year. Only progressively did I see that this continuity appears either in larger theme sequences or in subtle pointers from one verse to the next. This appendix will refer to these two helpers for those who enter the Calendar anew, or have little experience of it.

Spring

The first verse announces thinking reaching to the realm of cosmic life (spirit life) and dimly binding man's being to it. The second verse immediately follows by showing that thinking has completed its task and that it is "losing self-confines." Verse 2 has announced that the human being must find the fruit of soul within. It is through the ultimate effort of enlivened remembrance that the human being does this; in calling forth memory of its primeval paradisiacal state in the World All, and renouncing fetters of selfhood. The latter will become a theme from verses 3 to 6. The human being can now unite to this World All through the power of perceptive feeling which merges with the light of spring in verse 4. The theme of light forms the thread in verse 5 through the experience of resurrection from "narrow selfhood's inner power." And this resurrection forms the gate for the perception of the Self in verse 6. Verse 7 puts what seems a halt to this progression indicating that this Self can, yes, expand, but is thus risking losing itself in the "enticing light." Intuition is announced as the important future faculty of soul and as a theme that rises from verses 7 to 10.

In the next three verses the theme of intuition plays out in full force. Verse 8 restates the rise of the power of the senses and their threat for the soul, adding that thinking must recede to dreamlike dullness. Intuition asks the individual to forget the narrow will of self and lose itself in light in verse 9. In verse 10 intuition points the way to the goal of this forgetting and losing: let a godly being speak in the soul, inaugurating the theme of cosmic Word, implicit or explicit, in verses 10 to 13. It is this godly being which speaks in the next verse and asks the soul to lose itself to find itself in the cosmic I. The theme of losing itself in cosmic light and cosmic warmth is continued in verse 12 of Saint John; in verse 13 cosmic Word reveals itself explicitly and speaks offering the soul assurance that it can find itself in its true spiritual home, in the realm from where flame the words of truth.

Summer

That something important has occurred in this surrendering of the soul during spring is made clear by the emergence of the theme of selfhood in verses 14 to 16. The letting go of narrow boundaries of self gives way to the receiving of selfhood power. In verse 14 the reference to surrendering appears in negative with "dreamlike thinking seemed to daze and rob me of myself." Here the act of surrender is seen from the perspective of the lower ego as a loss. But the word "seemed" renders it clear that it is only a relative, apparent loss. In reality it is something that will serve the Self. Verse 15 already shows that this is not a loss but a process that takes time and trust on the part of the soul. The spirit world's enchanted weaving is surrounding the soul to let selfhood power emerge from a state of dormancy. Awakening from this state requires that the soul treasure and awaken to the realization of what it has been given by the spirit so that the gifts may bring forth "fruits of selfhood" (verse 16). The gifts are maturing in the depths of soul and in verse 17 we are asked to look at our inmost soul from where the cosmic Word can ring forth so that the Self be enriched by it. Aware of the presence of cosmic Word the soul summons the strength to expand and purify itself in verse 18. The theme of selfhood power that was in the background of verses 17 and 18 reemerges in verse 19 and continues in 20 and 21. Enriched by cosmic Word, our conscious effort to enliven its presence in our soul renders possible the emergence from the dream of summer. It enlivens the memory of what the soul has gone through in verse 19. This awakening is also providential in relation to the following, warning verse (20). We cannot just rest on what has been going on within the soul. We need to connect our ripened ego to the higher self by energetically turning to the world around us; from the dream of summer to the awakening call of Micha-el that is coming to us in the autumn air.

The threat to the Self which verse 20 has warned us about is averted in a gesture complementary to verse 7. The Self is, not surprisingly, felt as strange power, coming as it is from the realm of cosmic Self (21). Whereas the risk of spring was that of losing oneself in the external light, now the light becomes light of soul to nurture the human self out of the cosmic Self in verse 22. With the coming of autumn the gift of the summer light becomes light of soul, further nourishing the human Self. The light withdraws further from the external world to announce the summer of the soul in verse 23. In the same verse the theme of autumn-winter sleep is announced with the corresponding need to awaken. In verse 24 sleep is countered by strong inner activity; the theme is continued through to verse 26. The recognition of the Self at the center of the soul goes hand in hand with the rousing activity of Self-engendered will in verse 24. The light and activity inwardly generated now allow the soul to strengthen the Self and contrast the sleep of creation with the wakefulness of the soul in 25. The all-will Micha-el verse of 26 brings the cosmic life that has manifested in summer nature into the will and brings the Self to fathom the coming of Spirit Self in winter.

Fall

Michaelmas brought up the sense of Self as a goal for the season. In verse 27 I'm being asked to look into my being's depths where lies the Self as a gift of the summer sun. The theme of the sun becoming inner sun occupies the verses 27 to 30. In 28 I can feel my being vivified and renewed and with it the power of thinking, which, like the Self, comes from solar heights. The theme of thinking, overlapping with the inner sun, rises from verses 28 to 30. In verse 29 we are asked to fan its spark into flame with exertion of will so that in 30 the fruits of thinking are supported by the flow of feeling and bring about the "autumn's spirit waking" and "the summer of the soul." The theme of the Sun's power continues through the strengthening of the will in verses 31 and 32. In verse 31 this is expressed as forceful will of life leading to human deeds; in verse 32 the soul acquires inner certainty as to its presence in the world and its karmic relationships. This then naturally leads in verse 33 to the necessity for the soul to realize its responsibility in world's evolution and pledge to become a giver to the world. The world depends on human contribution for its sustenance and for its further evolution.

Verses 34 and 35 respond to the imperative of 33 with a strengthening of the Self. The vow of 33 leads to a newly risen sense of Self in 34, which can now wed the human being to the larger world through deeds in which are poured cosmic forces. The desire to mold self to true existence echoes in the yearning for knowing "being" and "true life" in 35, through which the Self can feel at one with the cosmic Self, with the Christ which is its true, and largest archetype. Verses 36 to 39 invite us into the realm of the cosmic Word, with a crescendo. In verse 36 the cosmic Self of 35 leads us to the cosmic Word residing in our soul and furthering our co-creative spiritual activity through the power of active sacrifice. Sacrifice becomes ultimately courage in verse 37, leading us to transform the world through the power of the cosmic Word.

To the theme of cosmic Word is now superposed that of heart and warmth from verses 37 to 43. To the awakening of the heart that we first see in 37 in the first winter verse (December 15 to 21) responds the gladness of heart at the birth of the spirit child within at Christmas. The cosmic Word wants to expand in joy out of the confines of our hearts. The spirit birth of 38 becomes spirit revelation in 39 which affirms the sense of Self out of the thinker's might. The fall quadrant of the year concludes with an affirmation of the light of thinking and warmth of heart which form the receptacle for the sense of Self, for the dialogue between Self and Spirit Self.

Winter

The light of the fall is tinged with warmth of heart for the first time at Christmas (verse 38). Now the light gives full way to winter warmth. Cosmic warmth of the height of summer is transformed at the opposite time of year into the warmth that we can generate in our hearts through the clarity of thinking and strength of Michaelic will. The first gesture of the cosmic Word within is one of cleansing. The soul can only make room to such resplendent presence if it can "fill the vain delusion of Self" with cosmic Word's power. The love that the I experiences in spirit depths (40) blazes through the soul with an imperative to flow into the world as human loving and working (41). The growth of the power of the heart now turns itself to the cosmos, bringing fulfilment to the imperative of verse 33 in 41 and 42. The warmth of heart of 42 defies the gloom of winter to become a force akin to that of nature, able to anticipate the sense-world's revelation. The forces of the heart are explicitly called upon once more, not just to anticipate the sense world's revelation, but to sustain and strengthen the world of appearances in verse 43.

Verses 44 and 45 remind us of the power of the spirit birth attained at Christmas, but now the focus changes with the purpose of preparing ourselves to the change that will be apparent in spring. While winter still offers us the experience of cold and darkness, the sphere of cosmic life animates all that is lying under the earth toward its future expression. Verses 44 to 49 bring the power of thinking to a culmination. The power of thought prepares to meet its counterpart in the forces of growth in the world. It equips the soul not to get lost under the stimulus of the senses and to meet these with assurance of its place in the world. The promise to meet the growth of spring with the creative will of thinking in 44 is echoed and enlarged with the light quality of thinking in 45, which will unite us with the world's becoming. The preparation that thinking has urged in the last two verses is now met as a threat to the forces of the soul in 46; something more is needed to join forces with thinking. That is the power of memory rising from spirit depths as a new source of inner light. We sense that this is a moment of balance between the two quadrants of winter and spring. While thinking is still growing, another faculty is emerging paving the way to the inner power of intuition of the later spring.

Verses 44 and 45 have announced the awakening of the powers of growth in the womb of the earth. Now thinking affirms itself by seeking and offering the human being a close union with the formative forces in nature, to which it is akin. Verse 47 reminds us of the necessity of being rooted in the growing strength of the power of thought. This strength is then met by the power of the light coming from the heights toward the soul. Thinking can become cosmic thinking that no longer reflects and separates but unites concept with percept and realizes their unity. From this cosmic thinking true freedom emerges that becomes capacity to love (48). Clarity of thought allied with memory's power generates hope in turning to the cosmic day with the gifts gleaned from the winter's cosmic night in 49. The light of winter carried into the spring becomes revelation and liberation in verse 50, with the concurrent expansion of the forces of cosmic life which will reach a climax in 52. Nature seeks itself in the human being. This is the attainment of the vow of verse 33. In verse 51 this powerful, but fleeting, revelation becomes for the human being the vow to seek itself beyond the play of the senses, to remember that it must seek for that part of the sense impressions that eludes normal consciousness, the spirit behind external appearance.

Verse 52 reminds us that with the approaching of the Christ mystery in outer nature the spirit seeks the human being just as much as the reverse. What flows from the universe as cosmic life seeks to unite itself with the human body, enriching its life forces. The movement is reversed at the turning point of the year (verse 1), when the Sun speaks to the human being and human thoughts reach to their primal cosmic source from which they will flow renewed throughout the spring and summer.

APPENDIX 2

_~~~ℳ~~~_

CALENDAR OF THE SOUL, FESTIVALS, EQUINOXES AND SOLSTICES

The Calendar of the Soul shows us a consistent pattern in relation to the main festivals of the year, those that are related to the equinoxes and solstices.

The Calendar of the Soul is written out of the sphere of the spiritual course of time itself, where dwell those beings whom Rudolf Steiner calls the Spirits of the Cycles of Time. It is the call of these beings that we must answer to, not the most external call of nature. In olden times there was a fuller alignment between cosmic beings and external nature. This is no longer the case as we have seen in the spring/summer dream and fall/winter sleep. At those times, as in the verses of cross 2, the calendar warns us not to just follow what outer nature would have us do. Here is a first sign of this emancipation from external nature. The same is reflected in the dates of the Christian festivals.

Easter emancipates the beginning of the year from the course of the Sun alone. Easter is in average three weeks after the Spring Equinox. It can be as close as one day after the equinox (March 22) or as far as five full weeks after (April 25). Because of this divergence at the time of the spring equinox, even after the adjustments that are taken before and after Easter, in order to bring about a coincidence with the time of Saint John, we witness that the apexes of the axes of the calendar are offset by one-two weeks from the fall equinoxes and solstices. This apparent anomaly reflects of the change between the pre-Christian and Christian festivals. We can see them one by one.

Saint John is no longer the time in which we are requested to go out of ourselves in ecstasy. This was the time that closely corresponded to the day of the summer solstice of old. The festival of Saint John is already placed three days after the solstice. And the attitude that is required of the human being is one of inner maturation, not one of sudden revelation. Emil Bock reminds us that Saint John should be seen as a preparation for the descent towards fall. And the old fires of ecstasy must be replaced by the fires of sacrifice. In future St. John will be the festival of the growth of Christ in us. The earth starts the inbreathing and this corresponds to the fact that we must turn inward and let the Christ in us grow. This can be done with an appeasement of the external fever of activity that accompanies summer.

The maturation of the assimilation of the gifts received from the macrocosm is reflected in the calendar in the fact that Saint John corresponds to week 12 of the calendar, not week 13 which forms the apex of the summer, together with week 14. This indicates the reality of the time of Saint John as a protracted season, not a single-day celebration.

As we move further along the seasons we arrive at the Fall Equinox. Here too we no longer have an exact correspondence with the festival that comes in average on verses 24 or 25. Michaelmas comes on the week following the equinox. Michaelmas corresponds to September 29th, and comes at the end of the summer quadrant of the calendar on verse 26th. The apex falls between verses 26 and 27. Michaelmas falls on the apex, but is further removed from the equinox. Here too we can argue that Michaelms is more than just a day celebration, but a festival mood that pervades the beginning of the Fall.

Finally, the circle closes at the time of the Winter Solstice. Christmas, just like Saint John, comes after the solstice. And the celebrations of Christmas really extend from the birth of Jesus to the birth of Christ, from December 25th to January 6th, thus including the days of the Holy Nights. Christmas is marked by verse 38th of the calendar, whereas the apex of the winter season comes in between verses 39 and 40, encompassing the Holy Nights. Here too it is the Christmas season that is emphasized, not just one day. The Holy Nights are a very special time of the year, reflecting of a new reality of the Christ-imbued Earth from the time of Golgotha.

Thus we can see the wisdom inherent in the Calendar of the Soul and its inner necessity in relation to the Christian festivals. This renders manifest why it was published in 1912, marking 33 years after the birth of the new Michaelic Age. The date of 33 AD as the birth of the Christ-I is crucial, because it reveals an important relationship between microcosm and macrocosm, in which Easter plays a central role.

APPENDIX 3

THE QUALITIES OF THE MID-SEASON QUADRANTS

Spring Equinox Quadrant:
Turning to Cosmic Life and Cosmic Light

Just as much as we have turned inward in the previous thirteen verses, now our soul gives itself to the movement of expansion brought about by the ethers' outbreathing that announces itself as we approach the time of the spring equinox. The whole of the verses 47 to 6 shows the soul's anticipation, preparation and adaptation to the rising of the spheres of cosmic life and cosmic light.

We are called to losing ourselves in nature consciousness, a realm not equal, but reminiscent of humanity's "original consciousness," to borrow Barfield's terminology. It differs in as much as we must retain ego consciousness while entrusting ourselves to the cosmos.

The verses have a pervading quality of wonder.

Verse 47
Already this verse sets the tone by announcing "the joy of growth ... quickening the senses' life." This, the verse says, is a situation that needs to be met by the strength of our thought and the cosmic powers that sustain it. The theme of thinking's affinity with the powers of life appears as one of many.

<u>Verse 48</u>

Thinking reaches an apex in cosmic thinking, uniting with love in human hearts. This thinking recognizes the force of cosmic light approaching the soul.

<u>Verse 49</u>

Having acquired cosmic thinking we can now recognize/sense cosmic life. The powers of memory allows us to recognize how thinking has matured in the absence of cosmic life, after the metamorphosis of cosmic life and cosmic light that has occurred in the soul. Now something approaches the soul from without with which it *feels* an inner affinity. Cosmic thinking can only approach the soul that has united itself with the Christ impulse.

<u>Verse 50</u>

Creation thanks the human being for its willingness to strive to reconnect, as the warning verse 46 enjoins us to do. The joy of growth can only penetrate the souls of those who have striven to redeem their thinking, those who want to co-create by letting nature recreate itself in human souls (verse 46).

<u>Verse 51</u>

The human I, that lives in wonder towards creation, offers this wonder to the macrocosm in every sense perception, and perceives more than what lives in the sense impressions. It renews its strength from the spirit hidden within nature, which otherwise is merely left out of the act of perception.

<u>Verse 52</u>

The I that turns in wonder toward the world wants to participate in the "life of worlds." The gaze of wonder receives beauty, and the conscious thinking human being unites with those creative formative forces which radiate strength into our bodies. This can only happen once the Christ impulse lives with elemental strength in our soul.

<u>Verse 1</u>

The maturation of the power of thinking allows a last recognition. Now it isn't just the macrocosm reaching to the human being as in verse 50.

Thinking, offered in joy, reconnects us to the formative cosmic forces, and our whole being feels transformed by the spirit.

Verse 2

Now that thinking has connected us to the cosmic formative forces, the Christ enlivened sphere of cosmic life seeks itself in the human being. In fact, we feel part of this reality, we grow into it to the point that we must remind ourselves that we have to hold on to our identity, which we cannot relinquish when our faculty of thought wanes. We still have that power that verse 46 calls memory, as we can see in the next verse.

Verse 3

Through memory we recognize that this sphere of cosmic life that the Christ draws near us in the miracle of nature is also our original home. We can slightly forget ourselves because we can recognize a state similar to that of humankind's original purity and innocence. Memory becomes cosmic memory. The resulting recognition renews our desire to grow beyond the hindrances of our personality, to seek our true self.

Verse 4

We enter now into contact with the realm of cosmic light through our enlivened, perceptive feeling. And this new experience renews in us the desire to later unite thinking and feeling to recreate a conscious experience of union between microcosm and macrocosm. This is an intuition of things to come.

Verse 5

Light is intimately interwoven with life: it draws out germinating power into space. The so-called lower ethers actually encompass the higher ones: life encompasses light and warmth; light encompasses warmth. We are aspiring to meet with our higher self; at least to receive its inspiration, even if in this time of the year it cannot be complete, because it does not occur through thinking.

Verse 6

Through our desire to free ourselves from fetters of selfhood we receive an intimation of our higher Self, and the vastness thereof. At this time of the year that we can have a feeling for the sphere of the etheric Christ. Therefore we perceive the reality of our higher Self in Christ. But it is also the time in which we can start to lose ourselves in the pull of the ethers. Something else is missing that has not been announced yet: it will come in verse 7 to form a counterbalance.

Verse 7

The warning verse articulates what we are left to guess from verse 6; what we can perceive in 6 is somehow premature; it announces something to come that we have to work at making our own. The power of thinking needs to be replaced by what Karl König calls boding, and Hans Pusch calls intuition. The verse speaks of thinking waning and intuition rising. Intuition will counter this movement of continued expansion with the risk of loss of Self through the acquisition of an inner compass.

Summer Equinox Quadrant:
Taking in cosmic Warmth and cosmic Word

Verse 7 has warned us about the temptation of the Self to flee into the light. This has to be countered through "ahnung"/intuition.

As cosmic warmth and cosmic Word draw near, the soul enters in dialogue through intuition. It is a call and response of sensing what is happening in the cosmos, and what our soul asks of us. It is a delicate interplay, like a balancing act.

Trust is one of the pervading themes and tone of this quadrant. The tentative, exploring mood that is turned toward an inner listening, is not present in the verses before 7, or after 20. After 20 we return to a much more affirmative mode.

Verse 8

The soul resists the onslaught of the senses by trusting that there is something there that it can trust. It is the approach of godly being, for which we must make room.

The verse echoes verse's 3 mood of self-forgetfulness. Intuition asks us to trust cosmic warmth filling the soul, and to allow oneself to be lost in the light in order to find oneself again.

Verse 10
Godly being returns to our conscience. We are guided to Him by the Sun, which spoke at Easter. Intuition takes the form of presentiment of future knowledge. Cosmic Word is perceiving us at present and we will realize this later in the summer. For now we just have to trust.

Verse 11
The soul divines words of wisdom guiding it to its next steps. In our ability to perceive beauty, just like we did in the week before Easter, the sun will guide our feeling life. We can trust the future will soon reveal the meaning of this time.

Verse 12
Having felt the beauty of the world we now sense an inner call to follow this movement of expansion done in trust. Our fledgling god-given powers want to expand into the cosmos and there allow me to find myself in cosmic light and cosmic warmth.

Verse 13
After following our inner promptings in the previous verses we can now hear a response sounding powerfully from the cosmos into the receptacle of our soul. It is the cosmic Word flaming with urge, out of the fiery worlds of the first hierarchy, enjoining us to seek ourselves in grounds of spirit. This is a pinnacle and turning point as we start descending from the St John mood toward the fall.

Verse 14
As we take stock of what happened ever since verse 8, we still need to trust beyond the appearance of having "lost the drive of our own being." On the contrary, we can realize it is our vigorous inner sensing, and trust in the benevolent powers of the cosmos, that has brought us to the place of recognizing cosmic thinking approaching us. Now begins a time in which

everything that was received from the cosmos is processed, refined and metamorphosed in the soul.

Verse 15

The soul can gratefully acknowledge a power higher than its own. With trust we can let this enchanted weaving, manifest in the power and glory of external nature, envelop us and bring to birth new powers in the soul. We sense the transition to a new feeling of Self, made possible by the soul's conscious desire to overcome the ego's narrow bounds.

Verse 16

Once more we are called to modest, quiet receptivity. It is a higher form of activity to follow the mandates of our voice of conscience, which tells us to treasure all that we have received, and trust that it will mature and bring about a new, fuller expression of selfhood.

Verse 17

What we have been waiting for, what has already expressed itself in different ways, now offers a resounding confirmation: "It is I, the cosmic Word, which have been approaching you through the portal of the senses, and can now announce myself." Receiving cosmic Word asks our soul to expand to larger "world-horizons."

Verse 18

We can follow the inner logic of the verses' sequence in verse 18. What cosmic Word asks of us, compels the eager soul to a commensurate response. Out of my inner being I must find the strength to purify and expand my soul for such a tremendous gift as that of cosmic Word.

Verse 19

Verse 19 brings a whole to a completion. The two powers that have accompanied us through the spring and summer—memory and intuition—now work at a new synthesis. It is fitting that we look back at the steps taken under the call of intuition to the promptings of the cosmos. This receptivity will lead to stronger forces of the Self wanting to emerge, since we were willing to sacrifice our lower nature.

Fall Equinox Quadrant: The Transformation of Cosmic Life and Cosmic Light

Between verses 20 and 33, both part of cross 7, the poetic language of the calendar indicates in every single verse the transformation of the ethers in ways that are not visible, neither before 20, nor after 33. This is a subtle interplay between heights and depths in which cosmic life and cosmic light, mutually influencing each other, are transformed into self-engendered will and light of thinking.

Cosmic life appears internalized in expressions such as "seed maturing" (21), "darkness of the soul" (24) a "seed" and "germinating force of soul" (27), "cosmic spirit fount of strength" (29), "forceful will of life" (31). Cosmic light appears transformed in a variety of expressions: "expectation, light-filled" (21), "light of soul" (22), "carry wakefully sun's glowing" (25), "gift of summer sun" (27), "sunlight of my soul" and "summer of the soul" (30).

The verses have a willful, affirmative quality to them.

Verse 21

The light coming from the cosmos is transformed into "light of soul." And this light of soul shines into spirit depths to bring about the maturation of the "human Self." The light that becomes inner light shines in the darker layers of the spirit, those that are less accessible to consciousness in which lives the will. The light brings to birth something new in the deeper soil of the soul. Light and life are now the light of soul and spirit depths where new growth germinates.

Verse 22

The verse continues the theme of light and the birth of the new in the depths of the soul. Here it is intuition/expectation offering its light to let the seed of selfhood's power come to maturation.

Verse 23

A process comes to completion. The external light wanes; the liveliness of the senses accompanies it in a similar movement. What is left is just a promise for the future. What ceases outwardly—the summer of the senses— becomes an inner summer of the soul. After this verse there will be no further reference to external light or life.

Verse 24
Here soul life emerges to bring about a birth from the depths of soul; that of Self-engendered will. The will emerges as a seed from the darkness that is illumined by the light of the Self, once more a transformation of cosmic life and cosmic light.

Verse 25
The reference to the external world is that of negation: darkness of space and time and sleep of creation. Within the soul, where the seed of the will and of the renewed Self has emerged, thinking, mentioned for the first time, can bring its shining inner light. It can carry the sun's radiance into the realms of cold, sleep and darkness.

Verse 26
Verse 26 renders explicit the link between Nature's maternal life/cosmic life that emerged out of the "world's great womb" (47) and the will's fiery energy. It announces the desire to strive for the fullness of the Self, and the Spirit Self that will be felt at Christmas time.

Verse 27
Intuition makes its last appearance to confirm that its role has been reached. The Self, a gift of the summer sun, is surrounded by the enveloping gesture of intuition, that offers it warmth and envelops it like a seed. Once more, light and life have been internalized and transformed into summer sun and seed.

Verse 28
Radiant, life-filled thinking emerges in its throne, so to speak. It takes central place in the landscape of the soul. It becomes its inner sun which casts light into the mysteries of life and offers hope in places where this had vanished. The whole inner being feels enlivened and widened.

Verse 29

Thinking has to become a flame, which for the first time announces the later transformation of cosmic warmth. Life is connected to the cosmic spirit's fount of strength. And this is explicitly stated as the summer heritage. Everything that came once from the cosmos to the human being, is now internalized and the human being is ready to radiate it out.

Verse 30

This is a verse completely dedicated to the inner light. Thinking becomes the sun of the soul. It brings about certitude of the Self's presence and growth. The inner light becomes joy and certainty of the future full summer of the soul. The strength of verse 29 becomes quiet inner certitude.

Verse 31

This is one of the light verses of cross 5. It announces what we have been surmising from the previous verses. What has been inwardly growing can no longer be contained. The light that has grown from spirit depths becomes in us forceful will of life that wants to express itself in human deeds. The growth of the conscious self and of the light of thinking announce the striving to bring the internalized cosmic forces to bear in the external world.

Verse 32

In this verse is one more expression of cosmic life, illuminated by thinking. Whereas in the previous verse light becomes life and will, here the strength and power we have acquired shines light in the form of insight into matters of destiny. It is another example of how cosmic life and cosmic light, become self-engendered will and thinking, continue to fructify each other.

Verse 33

It is fitting that what has been left behind, the world of nature that has sunk into sleep, cold and darkness, is now fully experienced but from within. We understand that we need to commune with the world of nature and recreate it in our souls for cosmic/human evolutionary purposes—that the external world depends on what the human being can bring out from within.

Winter Solstice Quadrant: Individualizing Cosmic Warmth and Cosmic Word Through Conscious Participation

The period is framed between verses 33 and 46. In 33 we are warned that the world depends on us for its further evolution. In 46 we realize that, because of a change of direction in the macrocosm the forces of the soul threaten to separate.

What has been internalized through the fall equinox time is now elaborated within through the contributions of cosmic warmth and cosmic Word. Thinking is further transformed and from it the human being develops the possibility to love selflessly.

Cosmic warmth re-emerges gradually as the new soul faculty of love. We encounter it in a variety of expressions in which warmth is internalized, starting with the first references to the heart: "my heart is ardently impelled" (34) "heart-high gladness" (38), "love-worlds of the heart" (40), "heart's own core", "kindle and inflame", "human loving" (41), "warmth of heart" (42), "glowing warmth", "forces of the heart" and "inner fire" (43).

In all the verses of this period the human being is turned inward to discover and strengthen a cosmos within, to acquire new faculties in order to become co-creator in the order of existence. We are called to take part in the world's evolving in what Owen Barfield would call "conscious participation."

Verse 34
We are calling on our Spirit Self through our "sense of Self" thanks to all that the soul has encountered in the fall solstice quadrant. We are confident that we can enter the world in a fuller way; we can now bring cosmic forces into our deeds.

Verse 35
The yearning for true being and true life becomes longing to find our Spirit Self in the cosmic Self. In our true being in Christ our Self acquires its fuller meaning. This brings "true life ... in the soul's creative urge."

Verse 36

What is announced in our cosmic Self becomes the wider, more encompassing cosmic Word/Logos. It is from this source that our presence in the world has fuller impact. It is from this union that we can feel able to sacrifice our lower self in service to the world. The theme of the cosmic Word now rises in the following verses.

Verse 37

Sacrifice awakens the forces of the heart, and what the human being pours out of the heart becomes seeds of soul which, through cosmic Word, have the power to transform. Verses 36 and 37 introduce the inner transformation of cosmic warmth through sacrifice and the impulses of the heart. What has acquired strength in the soul naturally wants to become presence in the world.

Verse 38

The Christmas verse marks the spirit birth (spirit child) of the cosmic Word in our hearts. The joy and warmth accompany the soul's desire to bring hope into and renew the world out of an overabundance of heart forces.

Verse 39

That Christmas is a spirit birth is confirmed in this verse. The spirit's revelation of the previous weeks has given depth to our thinking life, and given ground and reality to our Spirit Self. It has given us "light of cosmic being."

Verse 40

Cosmic warmth and cosmic Word now have a cleansing effect on our soul. The fire of love of the cosmic Word, moving through the heart purifies us of all "vain delusions of myself." This new impulse sets the tone for the following weeks. The inner freedom developed by "thinker's might" is transformed in our capacity for selfless love.

Verse 41

In this verse our newly developed love forces "kindle and enflame God-given powers." It's as if the human being, willing to sacrifice, moved to transform, can do no other than turn to his fellow human being through "human loving and human working."

Verse 42

What has touched our fellow human being in verse 41 moves further into the macrocosm. The light and warmth within are forces that resist the external forces of nature, which bring the darkness and "shrouding gloom." We have truly created a cosmos within which does not reflect external conditions. It anticipates and lives in the future, in the senses' revelation that is to come.

Verse 43

The warmth becomes inner fire of elemental strength. Our "true spirit-life" has cosmic formative power. We can defy the external world of cold and darkness with new power. We are no longer anticipating, as in the previous verse; we can now "give the world of appearance … the power to be."

Verse 44

The macrocosmic changes leading to warning verse 44 are now announced as a challenge, witness the word "bewildering" referring to the "world's sprouting growth." The challenge of the macrocosm is met in our microcosm through our "spirit-birth attained" and the "creative will of [our] thinking." We can continue to be co-creators because we have in our thinking a strength that matches that of the macrocosmic forces without. Our soul faculties will have the strength needed to preserve their unity.

Verse 45

This verse is a summation of the winter's journey. It is because we have achieved spirit birth at Christmas and because of the power of our forces of thought that we can pour these forces into the revelation of the senses. We can confidently "desire union with the world's becoming." In effect this announces the sphere of cosmic life approaching through Christ before and around Easter time.

MONTHLY VIRTUES IN RELATION
TO THE CALENDAR VERSES

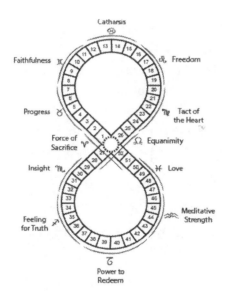

SPRING

The following section explores the Soul Calendar in relation to the virtues of the month, as they have been given in very short form by Steiner, and further elaborated in the work of Herbert Witzenmann. Mindfulness to the virtues of th month can help us strengthen our work with the calendar.

April: verses 51 to 2 (March 21 to April 21)
Devotion becomes force of sacrifice (Against lack of concern, spring fever)

Key words and expressions in the Calendar for this month are: spirit source (51) beauty, strength of life (52), the sun speaks, gladness (1) finding fruit of soul within ourselves (2)

As the power of the senses threatens to overwhelm us we receive the gift of strength of life uniting the spirit's being with human life (52) and binding the human being to the spirit's life (1) just as the power of thinking loses self-confines (2). We develop the ability to find the fruit of soul (2) without losing ourselves in the wide spirit world.

Verses 51 and 2 have a warning quality for the development of an extra effort in realizing the illusion of the senses (51) and the need to exert new inner faculties (2). Devotion is this capacity to turn inwards, welcoming beauty and developing gladness, and finding the fruit of soul within, supported by the strength of life streaming out of heaven's distances and the spirit's life bound up with our being.

Devotion to beauty and cosmic life, openness to the cosmos offer an opportunity for rebirth, but only if the soul opens up in a cultivation of devotion. This allows it to recognize the deed of Christ and to unite with His impulse.

May: verses 3 to 6-7 (April 21 to May 21)
Inner Balance becomes progress (against being taken up in externals and busyness)

There are a number of polarities that appear in these verses:

-   fetters of selfhood/narrow limits and true being/revelation of all worlds (3, 5, 6)
-   perceptive feeling and thinking's clarity (4, 7)
-   human being and world (4)
-   archetype divine / own likeness (6)

The integration of the polarities proceeds with a certain expansiveness from 3 to 5; it overshoots itself in verse 6, calling for a warning and compensation in verse 7, when intuition is called to establish balance and lead us into the next month beyond the Luciferic allure of losing ourselves in a movement towards ecstasy. Here we see the need for progress.

After the readjustment of the slightly warning quality of verse 2 and the risk of losing balance of verse 6, the soul finds itself all of a sudden in a great movement of expansion and change, and needs to find a balance through intuition/boding.

June: verses 7 to 11 (May 21 to June 21)
Endurance (perseverance) becomes faithfulness (against loss of grip / giving up)

The tendency to lose oneself in the senses and a macrocosmic bliss is countered by intuition/boding. What comes through the senses is a gift only if we can integrate it through inner activity. Intuition is announced in 7; in 8 we are told that we are entering a state of dream (dreamlike dullness and quiet dream life). This means that we are receiving from the cosmos: godly being desires union with my soul in 8; cosmic warmth fills all my soul and spirit in 9; the sun takes my human feeling into wide realms of space in 10. But to this must answer human activity. We are asked to lay human thinking content in quiet dream life in 8; to lose ourselves in light to find ourselves in 9; to awaken to the presentiment of a divine presence in 10; to struggle to understand the words of wisdom of 11. Faithfulness manifests itself in continuous inner activity and in refusing to let the externals take over, or losing sight of the goal. To listen to the voice of intuition requires trust and willingness to pass through unknowing with faithfulness.

SUMMER

July: verses 12 to 15 (June 21 to July 21)
Selflessness leads to catharsis (against self-absorption and willfulness)

Witzenmann calls this the time of "initiation into the path of destiny" and "transformation of the dangers which threaten the human creative center." The verses denote a continuous dedication to something larger than ourselves: "trustingly seek myself in cosmic light and cosmic warmth"

(12); "living in senses' heights" (13); "losing the drive of my own being (14). To this responds an agent capable of bringing about purification: cosmic light and cosmic warmth in 12; gods own word of truth in 13; the approaching of cosmic thinking in 14; the enchanted weaving of spirit within outer glory in 15. Purification is thus a continuous active entrusting of the human being to larger, cosmic forces. This is crowned and confirmed in 15 in which we are told that the enchanted weaving can bestow the strength that the I in its narrow bounds is incapable to give itself. The above are the antidotes against self-absorption and willfulness.

In verse 15 the human being can accept true selflessness in letting cosmic thinking "think us through": in accepting a call of destiny which can render us larger than our earthly ego; in letting our inner being reemerge anew through the help of the spiritual world.

Verses 13 to 14 move us toward powerlessness. I seek in spirit grounds; cosmic thinking approaches me in sense appearance. This is the step from letting go to letting the cosmic Word purify us through our willingness.

August: verses 16 to 19 (July 21 to August 21)
Compassion leads to Freedom (against heartlessness, lack of sensitivity)

Witzenmann reminds us that in compassion we reach a form of cognition in which we don't exercise, nor succumb to power. It liberates those whom it embraces, offering freedom.

Verses 16 to 19 show us a dialogue between Self and cosmic Word. Verse 16 starts with the injunction of "bearing in inward keeping spirit bounty"; verse 19 to "encompass with memory." The four verses stir the soul to energetic inner response: to bear in inward keeping (16); imbue my spirit depths with the cosmic Word wide world-horizons (17); find the strength to fashion worthily my soul (18); encompass with memory (19). The object of these efforts is to unite with cosmic Word (18) and ask the selfhood forces to give us to ourselves (19). This is how inner freedom finds expression.

In these verses I want to show myself worthy of what I have received. The receiving of cosmic Word is followed by its treasuring (16); thus cosmic Word can speak (17) and the I can strive to become worthy (18) and lastly hold everything in memory. (19)

When cosmic Word has found room in our soul, we need to accept the new tasks set up for us by cosmic thinking. The purification and cleansing of the soul gives us freedom from our lower self.

September: verses 20 to 24 (August 21 to September 21) Courtesy becomes Tactfulness of the Heart (against lack of consideration, carelessness)

Witzenmann speaks about experiencing the higher nature of the other person within ourselves; of continuously transforming the imperfect. He tells us that tact of the heart asks nothing of itself; it wants to assist other people in fulfilling their social-artistic tasks.

The verses start with the change of relation of knowing our life's reality in relation to the world's existence. The heart sensing is developed through: light-filled expectation working around selfhood power (21); the macrocosmic light becoming light of soul working into spirit depths (22); the spent summer giving itself to me (23); self-cognition and self-engendered will (24).

What these verses are speaking about is the culmination of the faculty of intuition (heart sensing) which educates our will towards truly living (self-engendered will) and ability to shed light into spirit depths. This is the culmination of the cycle of the summer, just before Michaelmas. The light without decreases, the light within increases. This becomes an impetus for wakefulness, self-cognition and effort of the will.

Intuition works at establishing balance between self and world (20) and what comes from the future. The ultimate desire of intuition is to respond to what comes from the future and this means sensing what needs to happen. In this instance the highest achievement of intuition is to listen to the voice within that tells us that the self needs to emerge and that another force will promote it. Intuition does this in verses 21 and 27, enthusiastically accompanying the new force of thinking. Tactfulness of the heart is about making room for what needs to happen.

Spring and summer develop in us virtues for receiving the world within us. These are virtues that give us to the world of nature and the presence of the spirit. We hollow ourselves out to become containers. This requires willingness to surrender, to purify ourselves and to make room for what the future calls into being.

FALL

October: verses 25 to 28 (September 21 to October 21)
Contentment leads to equanimity (against dissatisfaction and complaining)

Witzenmann contrasts desperate need with vision; this gives birth to the ability to overcome the "fear and horror in the face of events which press in from the future." And we know that this is exactly what Michael calls us to face.

Contentment is expressed in: I can belong now to myself and spread my inner light into the dark (25); steel my spirit striving to hold me in myself (26) find myself self-contemplating (27) radiance of my thought granting fulfilment to wishes lamed by hope (28). The depth of the will generated by tactfulness of the heart has let emerge a self that can now be supported by the radiance of thought.

The verse of Michaelmas is all life and will. The self emerges in 26 and in 27 it becomes a germinating force of soul. In 28 appears the first mention of the radiance of thought, which is the force that assures equanimity. This is the very Michaelic quality needed in entering the yearly time of darkness and the external darkness of civilization.

Verses 25 to 28 call to an awakening of hope and willed thinking. Equanimity lives in holding the balance between darkness and light, sleep and wakefulness (verse 25); seeing nature dying around us and nurture what grows inside (gift of summer sun). It holds that by necessity what dies without gives birth to new forces within; it gives equal stress to what is dying and what is coming to life. This is triumphantly asserted in verse 28: I feel my being vivified anew, / Widen to far horizons of its own. / Filled with new force the radiance of my thought. … Thus the human being can recognize with confidence the seed growing, even in the middle of cold and darkness.

November: verses 29 to 32 (October 21 to November 21)
Patience becomes insight (against hurry and loss of temper)

This is the month of Libra; the uniting of wisdom with strength; of knowledge fulfilling itself in activity. Acting out of spiritual cognition requires patience, from which arises insight. In Witzenmann's words: "Above the pillars of strength and wisdom of the apocalypse shines insight."

Verse 29 balances the strong inner activity of thinking with the ability to "read life's inner meaning out of the cosmic spirit fount of strength." Thinking and the flow of feeling support each other in verse 30, another sign of balance, leading to spirit waking. In 31 light and forceful will of life allow creative powers to ripen into human deeds. Verse 32 brings together strength to give me to the world with insight towards the weaving of life's destiny; it echoes what 29 set forth to accomplish. Insights generate understanding of the forces of destiny and desire for deeds, balance between wisdom and strength (verses 29 and 32).

Verse 29 is projected toward the future; it cherishes winter hope. Verse 31 looks forward to creative powers to ripen into human deeds. And 32 is affirmatively and fully in the present with knowledge of what is to happen.

> I feel my own force bearing fruit
> And gaining strength to give me to the world.
> My inmost being I feel charged with power
> To turn with clearer insight
> Towards the weaving of life's destiny.

December: verses 33 to 37 (November 21 to December 21)
Control of Speech becomes feeling for truth (against talkativeness, gossip)

Control of speech is what allows us to rise from mere subjective opinions to perceiving the essence of things. Control of the tongue leads to feeling for the truth. And this is expressed in the interchange between human being and world. Self knowledge leads to knowledge of the world; knowledge of the world to self-knowledge.

Warning verse 33 calls for the communion of my soul with the world's

161

reality. Verse 34 deepens my sense of self in order to pour cosmic forces into my deeds and find "true existence." To know myself I want to make my self at home within the cosmic Self (35). The cosmic Word unites my labor's aims with its bright spirit light and calls for my sacrifice (36). It is my task to awaken cognition ("carry spirit light into world-winter-night," and let "cosmic Word transfigure life"). And true knowledge, rather than opinion, becomes a creative force for world transformation.

The cosmic Word gives us a feeling for truth through its revelation and gives the human being alignment in his deeds. The spirit light that the cosmic Word offers in 36 becomes what I offer to the world through the heart in verse 37.

Truth awakens in the mind, but the feeling for truth has to be rooted in the heart. It is carried by the sense of Self (34). Truth is allied with the desire for full development of self. This striving calls the response of cosmic Word and alights the heart that wants truth to a new experience of being. Truth is only such if we are willing to be changed by it. The striving for cosmic Word in us is a striving for truth because it is a yearning to become more fully ourselves: "mold me into true existence" in 34; "can I know what it is to be" in 35, and "sacrifice myself through cosmic Word" in 36.

WINTER

January: verses 38 to 42 (December 21 to January 21)
Courage becomes the power to redeem (against timidity and anxiety)

Witzenmann comments that in the stream of the past we carry the urge to bring karmic compensation to where we have strayed from our path; in the capacities we have developed we meet the stream of the future. From the two comes acceptance of destiny which frees courage and gives us consciousness of immortality and ability to redeem.

In 38 the cosmic Word has engendered the heavenly fruit of hope in my soul core at Christmas. From thinking emerges the sense of Self, which deepens my courage (39). The cosmic Word takes root in my heart and frees me of delusions of self (40). It is in my heart (cor/cardium) that I develop courage. The heart's own core is mentioned again in 41 and with it the soul shaping itself in loving and working. It is warmth of heart in

162

42 that allows me to manifest my innate strength at the time of deepest darkness, and live with foreknowledge of the sense-world's revelation (42).

Verse 38 reminds us of the spirit birth of the cosmic Word. In 39 it becomes spirit revelation apprehended by the power of thought that strengthens sense of Self. This generates in 40 the cosmic warmth in the heart, freeing love and courage to understand and overcome "the vain delusion of my self." The courage unleashed in the heart kindles and enflames us for loving and working in 41. In verse 42 the contrast between outer darkness and inner light and warmth, impels the soul to find the strength to go into the darkness with courage and anticipatory hope, contributing to the sense-world's revelation.

February: verses 43 to 46 (January 21 to February 21)
Reticence becomes meditative strength (against comment and criticism)

Discretion (reticence) leads to the reversal of the way of thinking (metanoia), the opposite of the surrender to the senses. Through it the soul takes hold of itself as a citizen of the spiritual world. Discretion becomes meditative force.

Verse 43 indicates that true spirit life gives the world of appearance the power to be. The creative will of my own thinking prevents me from losing myself in new sense enticements (44). The verse restates both the light of thinking and the spirit birth, and adds to it the yearning of our soul. This leads to union with the world's becoming, the hallmark of meditative strength, which summons memory from spirit depths and strength of will for spirit sight when the world threatens to stun the forces of the soul (46).

Forces of the heart (43) work with the creative will of my own thinking (44). Heart and head work together so that the soul can seek union with the world's becoming. Inner force is created that can withstand the onslaught of the world on the forces of the soul.

The verses of the month speak of inner strengthening and union with the world's becoming. They emphasize how the world's evolving depends on the human being's inner strengthening. Meditative force enables us to strengthen ourselves and the world. Thinking, so concentrated as in the affirmation of the spirit birth, is a world changing power, yet it is all exerted from within. Verse 43 affirms this; true spirit life "gives to world appearance through forces of the heart the power to be." (43) And memory, willed from within, gives us the power to withstand "the world threatening to stun the inborn forces of the soul." (46)

March: verses 47 to 50 (February 21 to March 21)
Magnanimity becomes love (against pettiness and narrow mindedness)

What is true of the personal (meditative strength) now extends to the world around me (love). Magnanimity, which is full of interest and respect, creates a space in itself for all manifestation of being. It allies itself in freedom with each individual who strives, and becomes love.

Verse 47 challenges us to look at the approach of cosmic life and how the forces of the soul can disperse in the World-all and in the enticing light. Love manifests in desire for union with the world's becoming through strength of thought. Cosmic thinking approaches us now in full consciousness (contrary to the summer). The self fully sees the soul—of self and others—and love is awakened (48). Union with the world's becoming (and with other souls) turns into ability to feel the force of cosmic life and enkindle hope (49). The world now pours revelation into the human ego. Participation takes on a further step. This is knowing in the Biblical sense of union ("and Joseph knew Mary").

Verses 47 and 50 indicate the sphere of life; verses 48 and 49 that of light. Light moves more and more into life; it becomes the avenue for participation with the forces of life and for life to express itself in the human being. It is love in the human being that ultimately allows nature to speak to the individual in revelation and attain its true being (50). Cosmic life and cosmic thinking unfold in revelation and awaken love. Magnanimity lives in the soul having made room for the world and for other human beings; the soul who wants to widen its confines. The world of nature becomes one with us in our soul. We are fully reaching to co-creation before the primeval realm of cosmic life speaks to us again through Christ.

Reviewing the Virtues of the Year

Fall and Winter are times for developing virtues with which to meet the world and add ourselves to the work of creation. The tone is set by the Michaelic equanimity, which faces the world challenges with assurance and strength. The rising power of thinking manifests itself in insight, feeling for truth and meditative strength. Courage allied with the light of thinking becomes love at the turning point of the calendar. This is love for the world and for the Christ impulse which gives it full meaning. The capacity to sacrifice ourselves consciously through cosmic Word (36) sets the tone through spiritualized thinking for the achievement of love.

At the two ends of the year two completely different gestures are called into being. In spring and summer we recognize selfhood's fetters and the narrow limits of self. This opening of self to the world is aptly called forth in April when devotion becomes force for sacrifice. There is no opening of the ego to the cosmos without this inner attitude. The end result of the soul's progress through spring and summer is the virtue of tactfulness of the heart. Boding has developed inwardly as the capacity to enter in dialogue with self and world and to decipher the forces of destiny; to be able to sense what comes to us from the future; a higher sensing of the heart.

In fall and winter the soul opens to the renewed capacity of thinking. For this purpose nothing is more apt than to begin with the development of equanimity (September); the soul's ability to receive without judgment everything that approaches it from without. Thinking has to accept everything with equal value before it can re-order and discriminate. When thinking is brought to its ultimate destination, when it is spiritualized, it brings the human being to a new place in the world. Meditative strength opens the door to true freedom and love.

APPENDIX 5

NOTES ON THE CROSSES OF THE CALENDAR OF THE SOUL

The following are some evolving notes on the qualities of the quartets/ crosses of the Calendar of the Soul. The crosses are contrasted in terms of the soul forces they address most (thinking, feeling and will), the ethers to which they refer and their metamorphosed inner correspondent, their inner or outer focus, and their overall qualities.

Crosses 1 to 3 engage us primarily in the sphere of cosmic life and its metamorphoses in the soul.

Cross 1
The cross has a germinal quality of exuberance and of new beginnings. Central to it are such expressions as sprouting, fiery energy, spirit striving, germinating force. They mostly address the will. The verses of cross 1 are experienced in the year during two following weeks, since in the calendar we move from 1 verse of cross 1 to another one (from 52 to 1 and from 26 to 27). They are pivotal. In moving from one verse to another of cross 1 we experience a reversal from life to will, and/or from being to life.

Cross 2
After we are set on our course we now experience a change of direction and mild warning. The human being has to apply inner strength to create a change, an effort of will to engage in a new direction. The soul acts

contrary to what outer nature would induce it. It has to listen to the hierarchies behind the veil of nature. The inner Sun has to regulate the soul forces of thinking, memory, intuition, self-engendered will.

Cross 3

Here we can detect a quality of will: it's similar to a return to Cross 1 at a higher level of consciousness. We can strive to integrate strength and wisdom: strength to know (I) and to be known (nature). König calls these "verses [of] expression of the experience of the soul that relates to the course of time." We could say that we move from original participation, though different from what it once was before the Christ impulse, to more conscious participation.

Crosses 4 to 6 engage us in the realms of cosmic life and cosmic light and their soul metamorphoses.

Cross 4

These verses speak most to thinking and feeling. In this quartet we witness the journey of the light from without to within and then without again: from light to summer of the soul, to cosmic day. We encounter a balance between light and darkness. Two of the verses relate to Beltane and All Souls, times in which the soul can experience openness between worlds. And the verses mirror this with a desire to integrate the human being and the world. Notice that voices speak in verses 4 and 49: perceptive feeling and clarity of thought.

König qualifies the cross as the "archetype of what as a reflection takes place as human destiny: seeking, finding, separating and renunciation."[47] They do in effect reflect our journey from a state of separation to reconnection to our Father ground of existence.

Cross 5

These are the verses of the so-called "light cross." They present a strong contrast between the outer and inner, between spirit depths and worldwide heights, between germinating power in space and forceful will of life. They

---

[47] Karl König, *The Calendar of the Soul: A Commentary*, 96.

call strongly to the will. König sees in these a "Streaming of light from the soul into the world and from the world into the soul."[48]

Cross 6
The verses have a quality of intimation/anticipation/expectation. Here we witness power directly associated with the Self and the world. The light becomes inner light then insight and strength of thought. König sees in the verses "the self holding the balance between the lower and higher egos."

Cross 7
Here we see the announcement of the reversal of natural tendencies, calling for newly emerging or strengthened soul faculties, amplifying what we saw in cross 2. The verses announce the emergence of the four cardinal inner forces: memory, intuition, self-engendered will, thinking. They invite us to protect the self from the world in order for the self to pour itself out in the world in right relationship.

With crosses 8 and 9 we move from cosmic light into cosmic warmth, from thinking to destiny and love.

Cross 8
Cross 8 echoes cross 2; the verses indicate the need for a reversal to take place. They ask us to be prepared, to take a pause; they display a quality of determination and confirmation. They announce a step to be taken, that will change the relationship between macrocosm and microcosm. Intuition and thinking are presented in their clearest example.

Selfhood forces interplay with cosmic forces, through giving and receiving, and fructifying each other. The Self is strengthened, experienced and expressed. Through this strengthening we can give back to the world what has been received and made conscious.

Cross 9
These are verses about reaching for the reality of the Self. They lead us from trust to sacrifice, to participation in the spirit and perception of the spirit in matter. The Self gives us our true place in the world. Our moral

---

[48] Karl König, *The Calendar of the Soul: A Commentary*, 100.

striving yearns to lead us to selflessness. We are preparing the inner world to receive forces from the macrocosm.

Crosses 10 to 13 move us into the realm of cosmic Word

Cross 10
The verses call to feeling and will. We enter the sphere of cosmic warmth, Sun and forces of the heart (sacrifice, inner fire). The cosmic Word appears for the first time and changes our relationship to the Self and to world. The soul moves from acknowledging cosmic Word to acquiring the capacity to co-create. Three voices call us in verses 10, 17 and 36. In 10 presentiment announces what will be cosmic Word, which then speaks in 17 and 36.

Cross 11
Here the inner voice speaks directly and with a quality of command/resolve implying a will quality. We witness the further work of the cosmic Word in us. It speaks within and transforms soul and world. We experience processes of waiting, anticipating, maturing, transforming, and move from trust to resolve.

Cross 12
We could call this cross one of gestation and birth of cosmic Word in us. It calls us, protects us, gives birth within us, wanting to flow into the world. The spirit expresses itself in the Self and from it into the world.

Cross 13
With cross 13 we are fully in the sphere of cosmic light and warmth. Thinking leads to cosmic thinking and in the heart to loving. Cosmic Word becomes light of cosmic being and spirit revelation; matter expands to spirit or spirit concentrates in matter. This is the cross calling us to surrender and sacrifice.

As in cross 1 the verses of quartet 13 are experienced in the year during two following weeks, since in the calendar we move from 1 verse of cross 1 to another one (from 13 to 14 and from 39 to 40). Here too we see a reversal at play: from surrendering to seeking and vice-versa; from warmth to light and vice-versa.

Complementary Crosses

We can now look at the complementary qualities that the crosses display around the axis of cross 7. This forms the polarities between crosses 1 and 13; 2 and 12; 3 and 11; 4 and 10; 5 and 9; 6 and 8.

Crosses 1 and 13

These crosses form the polarities of cosmic light and cosmic life in 1, cosmic warmth and cosmic Word in 13. We see the beginnings of Self in 1; the culmination of sense of Self (Spirit Self) in 13. The two crosses indicate a reversal of direction: in 1 from life to will, and/or from being to life; in 13 from warmth to light and vice-versa, and from surrendering to seeking and vice-versa.

Crosses 2 and 12

Cross 2 is directed toward the change that has to happen inwardly in relation to human emancipation from nature: this denotes a quality of restraint, awakening. Cross 12 is directed outwardly towards the change that the human being can affect in the world: receiving cosmic Word and giving it out.

Crosses 3 and 11

Both crosses have qualities of resolve. Cross 3 offers us a new self-world relationship: it unites strength with knowledge. We are directed inwardly.

In cross 11 cosmic Word speaks in us, transforms the soul and the world. We are directed outwardly.

Crosses 4 and 10

Both crosses contain the mid-season festivals: cross 4 Beltane and All Souls; cross 10 Candlemas and Lammas.

In cross 4 we witness an interplay of feeling and thought. The voices of perceptive feeling and thinking speak to us.

The verses of cross 10 call to our feeling and will; the feeling becomes warmth and inner fire. Cosmic Word speaks twice; in verse 10 it is our soul who announces it.

<u>Crosses 5 and 9</u>

Cross 5 speaks of the gifts of light to us and of the inner light to the world. The verses denote an "active" will quality, outwardly directed.

The verses of cross 9 indicate a "receptive" quality of the will: an effort of the self to change the soul and through this affect the world. The effort is oriented inwardly.

<u>Crosses 6 and 8</u>

The qualities here cultivated are those of expectation, anticipation. In its connection self-world and self to self, cross 6 is outwardly oriented.

Cross 8 has a quality of determination and confirmation. In calling us to the development of new soul faculties it is inwardly oriented.

APPENDIX 6

THE CALENDAR OF THE SOUL IN RELATION TO THE PRACTICES OF THE FOUNDATION STONE MEDITATION

We have emphasized in this work how the Calendar of the Soul weaves in between the activities of the hierarchies in nature and in the cosmos—the macrocosm—and the corresponding responses of the soul ebbing and flowing during the seasons—the microcosm. We have seen the yearly rhythmical alternation of memory, intuition, self-engendered will, and thinking. We will now look at the contrast between spring and summer on one hand and fall and winter on the other in relation to the first three stanzas of the Foundation Stone Meditation, which is offered below.

The calendar as a whole forms a breathing between soul and cosmos; it is what brings the soul in balance with the course of the year, and ultimately with the place of the Christ being in the order of nature and the universe.

In the second panel of the meditation the practice of Spirit Mindfulness (or Spirit Awareness)—which is the only one directly related to the Christ in the meditation—emphasizes what the calendar accomplishes in many ways. It is the practice that through our middle being—that of heart and lung—takes us "through the rhythms of time into the feeling of our own soul being" and does so "in balance of the soul." In the calendar the rhythm is that of the year, which relates to the cosmic rhythms of Sun and Moon, through which the year's beginning is set at the changing date of Easter. In this we can see an expression of the "Christ will" that "holds sway in rhythms of time."

During spring and summer, memory builds the inner orientation and focus of the soul; it is its "inward sight." To this is added intuition, that capacity which in concert with memory/recollection teaches us to order our will, to bring thinking into our external activities. Altogether this is the acticity at the heart of the practice of Spirit Recollection, that König called boding, and that we have called intuition.

In the first verse of the meditation the practice of Spirit Recollection is that which we practice "in depths of soul" and through which we "live in the limbs." It places us in touch with the world of the soul, with the forces at play in our biography, which point to the karma we have generated through our earth incarnations. Through Spirit Recollection our "own I comes into being in the I of God" so that we can "truly live." The warm time of the year is that in which we need to find our response to the cosmos approaching us; we have to fathom it from the depths of our soul, through intuition and memory. Memory looks backward, intuition forward. We have to learn to truly live out of what we can bring out from the depths of our soul.

Here Spirit Recollection takes on a more encompassing nature from its usual term, because it includes not only the human being's biography but the events of the cosmos. Spirit Mindfulness adds through every verse its gesture of balance of the soul, weaving inner activity with events of nature and cosmos. Examples of this enlarging of boundaries in the Calendar include:

- Verse 10: a godly being now has touched you
- Verse 13: in spirit sources seek expectantly to find your spirit kinship
- Verse 18: can I expand my soul that it unites itself with cosmic Word

The gesture of Spirit Mindfulness is present in the way in which the calendar invites us to receive the gifts of the macrocosm without taking leave of ourselves. The soul cannot be lost in the external dream of the season; it has to find an inner compass. Once more the gesture of interweaving of above and below is present: the warm time of the year wants to take us beyond ourselves. While we receive the gifts of the macrocosm, we consciously turn our attention inward in order to integrate the gifts we receive and develop selfhood power. As we transition into the fall we can say, "I feel at last my life's reality," but also know that it cannot be "severed from the world's existence" (verse 20).

Moving into the fall the Michaelic—self-engendered will—directs us both to the needs of Earth and also to the personal dimension of our lives. Soon after Michaelmas this turns into what the calendar calls "the summer of the soul," the solar faculty of thinking, which "thrives in the sunlight of the soul." The two activities brought together indicate the pouring of the will into thinking, which is part and parcel of what the Foundation Stone Meditation calls Spirit Beholding.

In Spirit Beholding we are called to living "in the resting head" which "reveals . . . world thoughts" bestowing on us "world-being light" out of "the eternal aims of gods." The end result is being able to "truly think from the ground of the human spirit." Whereas Spirit Recollection is the gateway to the inner world of the soul, Spirit Beholding leads us into the macrocosm. Nevertheless the practice of Spirit Beholding, of the cold time of the year in the calendar, weaves between the macrocosm and the microcosm of our human relations as well. It is encompassed by the gesture of Spirit Mindfulness through and through. Examples of it:

- Verse 32: my inmost being I feel charged with power to turn with clearer insight toward the weaving of life's destiny.
- Verse 34: this shall, awakening, pour forth cosmic forces into the outer actions of my life
- Verse 41: the soul thus shapes itself in human loving and in human working

Come fall we see the world moving into apparent sleep. The soul is tempted to retreat into itself. The calendar calls for a vigorous exertion of the will turned outward, and toward seeking to develop sense of Self.

We are asked to take our role in the continuation of the work of creation; through this vigorous activity we can attain Imagination, then Inspiration and Intuition, those capacities through which we become citizens of the macrocosm. As winter approaches we "feel at last the world's reality" which needs "the communion of my soul" and needs "to recreate itself in souls" (verse 33).

The fourth stanza of the Foundation Stone Meditation anchors the meditation to the turning point of time, the event of Golgotha. It starts with "At the turning point of time the spirit light of the world entered the stream of earthly being." The same could be said of the Calendar of the Soul. Though never mentioned, the historical Christ event and the coming of Christ in the etheric determine the setting of the calendar at the time of Easter. The tone of the calendar, as it approaches its first verse, is set by the approaching of cosmic life that the Christ event has rendered a reality for Earth existence at the turning point of time.

In summing up, we see the three practices of the Foundation Stone Meditation alternate through the year. Spirit Mindfulness is always present throughout the year in the calendar's gesture of integration of the movements of the macrocosm and those of the soul. In spring and summer this is colored by Spirit Recollection, in fall and winter by Spirit Beholding.

Human Soul!
You live within the limbs
Which bear you through
the world
of space
Into the spirits' ocean-
being:
Practice spirit-recalling
In depths of soul,
Where in the wielding
World-Creator-Being
Your own I
Comes into being
In the I of God;
And you will truly live
In human world-all being.

For the Father-Spirit of
the
heights holds sway
In depths of worlds
begetting life.
Spirits of Strength:
Let ring forth from the
heights
What in the depths is
echoed.
Speaking:
Out of the Godhead we
are born.

This is heard by the sprits
of
the elements
In east, west, north,
south:
May human beings hear
it!

Human Soul!
You live within the beat of
heart
and lung
Which leads you through
the
rhythms of time
Into the feeling of your
own soul-
being:
Practice spirit-sensing
In balance of the soul,
Where the surging deeds
Of World-evolving
Unite your own I
With the I of the world;
And you will truly feel
In human soul's creating.

For the Christ-will
encircling us
holds sway,
In world rhythms,
bestowing
grace upon souls.
Spirits of Light:
Let from the east be
enkindled
What through the west
takes
on form,
Speaking:
In Christ death becomes
life.

This is heard by the spirits
of
the elements
In east, west, north,
south:
May human beings hear
it!

Human Soul!
You live within the resting
head
Which from the grounds of
eternity
Unlocks for you world-
thoughts:
Practice spirit-beholding
In stillness of thought,
Where the gods' eternal
aims
Bestow the light of cosmic
being
On your own I
For free and active willing.
And you will truly think
In human spirit depths.

For the Spirits' world-
thoughts
hold sway
In cosmic being, imploring
light.
Spirits of Soul:
Let from the depths be
entreated
What in the heights will be
heard.
Speaking:
In the spirit's cosmic
thoughts the
soul awakens.

This is heard by the spirits
of
the elements
In east, west, north,
south:
May human beings hear
it!

At the turning point of
time
The Spirit-light of the
world
Entered the stream of
earth
existence.
Darkness of night
Had ceased its reign;
Day-radiant light
Shone forth in human
souls:
Light
That gives warmth
To simple shepherds'
hearts;
Light
That enlightens
The wise heads of kings.

Light divine,
Christ-Sun,
Warm
Our hearts;
Enlighten
Our heads;
That good may become
What from our hearts
We are founding,
What from our heads
We direct,
With focused will.

177

BIBLIOGRAPHY

Bock, Emil,
- *The Circle of the Year's Festivals: A Collection of Essays* (manuscript available through Rudolf Steiner Library).

- *The Rhythm of the Christian Year. Renewing the Religious Cycle of Festivals* (Edinburgh: Floris Books, 2000).

König, Karl,
- *Rudolf Steiner's Calendar of the Soul, a Commentary*, (Rudolf Steiner Press, 1989).

- *The Calendar of the Soul: A Commentary* (from Karl König Archive) (Edinburgh: Floris Books, 2011).

Marti, Ernst,
- *The Four Ethers: Contributions to Rudolf Steiner's Science of the Ethers; Elements, Ethers, Formative Forces* (Roselle, IL: Schaumburg Publications, 1984).

Merry, Eleanor,
- *A Commentary* [to the Calendar of the Soul] in *Calendar of the Soul* with illustrations by Valorie Jacobs, translation by Ernst Lehrs (London: Rudolf Steiner Press, 1970).

Morelli, Luigi,

- *Karl Julius Schröer and Rudolf Steiner: Anthroposophy and the Teachings of Karma and Reincarnation* (Bloomington, IN: I-Universe, 2015).

Steiner, Rudolf,

- *Anthroposophical Leading Thoughts*: *A Christmas Study; The Mystery of the Logos*, 1924.

- *The Calendar of the Soul*, lecture of May 7th, 1912.

- *The Calendar of the Soul*, translated by Daisy Aldan (Spring Valley, NY: Anthroposophic Press, 1974).

- *The Calendar of the Soul by Rudolf Steiner with Translations by Daisy Aldan, John F. Gardner, Isabel Grieve, Brigitte Knaack, Ernst Lehrs and Ruth and Hans Pusch and a Paraphrase by Owen Barfield* (Spring Valley, NY: Mercury Press, 1999).

- *Christ and the Human Soul*, 1914.

- *The Cosmic Word and Individual Man*, lecture of May 2, 1923.

- *The Cycle of the Year as Breathing Process of the Earth*, 1923.

- *The Easter Festival in the Evolution of the Mysteries*, 1924.

- *Eight Lectures to Doctors*, 1924.

- *Esoteric Christianity and the Spiritual Leadership of Humanity*, 1911.

- *Four Seasons and the Archangels*, 1923.

- *The Gospel of St. John*, 1908.

- *Human and Cosmic Thought*, 1914.

- *The Inner Nature of Man*, 1914.

- *Theosophy*, 1904.

Zeylmans van Emmichoven, F. W.,
- *The Anthroposophical Understanding of the Human Soul*, (Spring Valley, NY: Anthroposophic Press, 1982).

Witzenmann, Herbert,
- *The Virtues: Contemplations* (New York: Folder Editions, 1975).

Printed in the United States
by Baker & Taylor Publisher Services